P9-EDE-254

Cooking with Jenn-Air

Cooking with Jenn-Air

A Benjamin Company Book

Jenn-Air consultants: Ann Vaughan
                       Gail Heeb
Home economics consultant: Betty Sullivan
Recipe development and testing: Barbara Bloch
                                 Freddi Greenberg
                                 Barbara John
                                 Alice Pearson
Color photography: Meryl Joseph
Cover photograph: Walter Storck
Illustrations: Tom Brecklin
Typography: A-Line, Milwaukee
Production manager: Beth Kukkonen
Copyright © 1980 Jenn-Air Corporation
  and The Benjamin Company, Inc. All rights reserved.
Published by The Benjamin Company, Inc
              485 Madison Avenue
              New York, N.Y. 10022
ISBN: 0-87502-072-0
Library of Congress Catalog Card Number: 79-54943
Printed in the United States of America

98765432

CONTENTS

Introducing

COOKING WITH JENN-AIR

When the Jenn-Air Corporation was founded in 1947 by Louis J. Jenn, its first products were improved ventilation devices for the restaurant industry. Today you'll still see Jenn-Air ventilation equipment being used by America's finest restaurants as well as in many worldwide commercial and industrial applications.

When Jenn-Air brought its ventilation expertise to the consumer by entering the residential appliance field, its first range and eye-level oven won the coveted "Best Design of a Consumer Product" award given every two years by the American Iron & Steel Institute. It was the first range with built-in ventilation, an exclusive, patented development of the Jenn-Air Corporation.

Over the years the Jenn-Air Corporation has been responsible for the introduction of many "firsts" for residential appliances. Our proximity (or surface) ventilation system, which makes indoor grilling possible, has long been a favorite of American and Canadian consumers.

When Jenn-Air introduced the "convertible cooktop," it was an immediate success. Convertibility made it possible for the user to have the menu flexibility of a fine restaurant at his or her fingertips. The cook of the house can, for instance, convert the range top to a grill in seconds and with optional accessories can expand the flexibility of this versatile range with a rotisserie, shish kebab accessory, non-stick griddle, or French fryer/cooker. It is America's *most* flexible cooking system.

In 1976, Jenn-Air introduced its first "selective-use" convection oven. Convection ovens, long popular with consumers in Europe and utilized by leading restaurants throughout the world, cook food in a stream of constantly recirculating heated air. Uncovered meat prepared in this heated air stream cooks faster and with less moisture loss than in a regular oven. Convection roasting assures the juiciest and most flavorful meat possible at home.

Rib Roast of Beef   *vii*
(Chart, page 72)

Unlike the majority of convection ovens available in the United States, the Jenn-Air "selective-use" oven recognizes that while the convection oven is superior for cooking most food, the conventional radiant-heat "bake 'n broil" oven is best for some other kinds of food, such as super-rich baked products. The Jenn-Air convection oven converts to a standard radiant oven at the touch of a switch. Consumers enjoy the best of both worlds without sacrificing food quality or appearance.

Cooking with Jenn-Air is our first major cookbook. It is designed to help you explore the many exciting and flavorful cooking adventures you'll enjoy with our "convertible cooktop" grill and accessories and with our "selective-use" convection oven. These recipes were developed to accent the many menu-expanding ideas that your Jenn-Air equipment will suggest day after day. They merely hint at the great flavors and variety possible when you cook with Jenn-Air.

This book is not necessarily a collection of all-time classic recipes, but rather new approaches to old favorites as well as many recipes created especially for your Jenn-Air equipment. All the recipes are designed to help you get more enjoyment from the equipment. We hope they will whet your appetite for developing your own culinary skills and the creative cooking approaches possible with Jenn-Air.

Jenn-Air is proud of its reputation as a manufacturer of creative and innovative cooking systems that meet the highest standards of excellence. That's what Jenn-Air is all about. Now it is time for you to explore the wonderful world of Jenn-Air as you let *Cooking with Jenn-Air* introduce you to a new world of flavor!

Cordially,

Ann Vaughan
Director of Consumer Services
Jenn-Air Corporation

Cooking with Jenn-Air

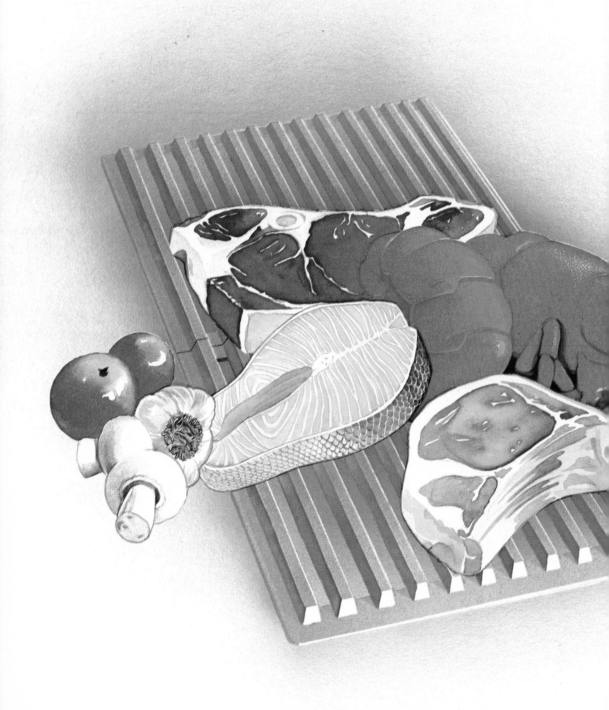

JENN-AIR GRILL

Your Jenn-Air grill can bring the outdoors inside. Now, with the convenience of indoor grilling, the food you usually grill outside can be cooked quickly and efficiently all year round.

Grilling is one of the most satisfactory methods for cooking many cuts of meat, many kinds of fish, poultry, and vegetables. For best results buy top grade meat and trim off all excess fat before grilling. Meat that is at least 3/4-inch thick will grill better than thinner cuts. Poultry and non-oily fish will probably need some extra fat; brush them with oil or melted butter occasionally during grilling.

The flavor of many foods is enhanced by grilling. Cook your next hamburgers and hot dogs on the grill. The buns can be heated right along with the meat. Roast corn on the cob would complete a feast. Because your Jenn-Air grill is vented by its excellent exhaust system, smoke and fumes will not be a problem. Occasionally there may be a

brief flare due to excessive fats, grease buildup, or other factors, such as improper ventilation. In case of a flare, turn off all heating elements, then manually turn on the "Fan." Flare-ups will be less of a problem if the grates and grill-rock elements under them are kept clean. Scrubbing with a stiff brush or plastic scouring pad and household detergent works well, and of course, a dishwasher makes clean-up easy. Never leave the grill unattended.

The grill will work best and be easiest to clean if you season new grates before you use them. Brush with a light coating of vegetable oil or a non-stick vegetable spray. You may want to use it each time you use the grill. Reseason grates after they have been washed. If you are grilling a small amount of food, steak for two people, for example, you can make use of the "energy-saver" feature of the grill (available on deluxe Jenn-Air grill-ranges) and heat only half the grate area.

Preheat 5 minutes on "HI" for best flavor.

| | | Setting | Approximate Cooking Time (minutes) | |
			First Side	Second Side
Steak	Rare	HI	5	4
(½-¾")	Medium	HI	6	6
	Well	HI	8	8
Steak	Rare	HI	5-7	5
(1-1½")	Medium	HI	9-11	10
	Well	HI	12-15	12

		Approx. Total Cooking Time (minutes)
Hamburgers (1/2"-5/8")	10	15-25
Hot Dogs	HI	5-10
Pork Chops	9	30-40
Barbecued* Spareribs	10	50-60
Lamb Chops	9	25-35
Chicken Pieces	10	45-60
Ham Slice	10	15-20
Lobster Tails	8	20-30
Garlic Bread	HI	2-3

*Baste with barbecue sauce last 15-20 minutes.

When basting meat or applying barbecue sauces to food, remember that excessive amounts only wind up inside your grill and do nothing to improve flavor. Sugar-based sauces used excessively can caramelize on the flavor-cartridges to create a cleaning chore.

For the attractive "branded" look on steaks, be sure grill is preheated. Let one side of meat cook to desired doneness, then repeat on second side of meat. Scissor-type tongs with long handles are ideal for handling meat such as steaks or chops.

Should broiled foods be prepared and ready before you're ready to serve, turn heat control to a low setting and cover meat with a single sheet of foil. Our advice is to have the guests ready when the broiled food is!

GRILLED HORS D'OEUVRE

Cut sausages in half. Cut spareribs into individual pieces. Wrap chicken livers with half slices of bacon and secure with wooden picks. Cut off wing tips and discard (or save to use in soup); cut through joint of chicken wing to make 2 small pieces. Lightly brush grill grates with vegetable oil. Preheat grill on "Hi" for 5 minutes. Place food on grill for 20 to 25 minutes, turning frequently. Serve with soy sauce, Sweet-Sour Sauce (page 58), Hot Mustard Sauce (page 96), or Barbecue Sauce (page 41) for dipping.

Note: All these appetizers can be prepared ahead and frozen. Place them on a freezer-proof tray and freeze until firm. Remove to an airtight container and return to freezer. The frozen hors d'oeuvre can be cooked directly on the grill as needed. Allow about another 10 minutes cooking time.

6 to 8 servings

1 package (8 ounces) sausage links
1 rack pork spareribs, cut crosswise through the bone
1 pound chicken livers
1/2 pound bacon
1/2 pound chicken wings

ANCHOVY SHRIMP APPETIZER

Shell shrimp; slit down back and remove vein. Cut anchovies in half lengthwise and put one piece of anchovy in the shrimp slit. Wrap shrimp in bacon; secure with wooden pick. Lightly brush grill grates with vegetable oil. Preheat grill on "Hi" for 5 minutes. Place shrimp on grill and broil 7 to 8 minutes on each side. Bacon should be browned and crisp. Serve hot.

16 servings

16 jumbo shrimp (about 1 pound)
1 can (2 ounces) anchovy fillets
8 slices bacon, cut in half

PEPPER STEAKS

Trim excess fat from steaks. Sprinkle each steak liberally with crushed peppercorns and press lightly into the meat. Pour the wine into a shallow casserole and add steaks and turn to coat with wine. Let stand at room temperature 30 minutes.

Lightly brush grill grates with vegetable oil. Preheat grill on "Hi" for 5 minutes. Place steaks on hot grill and broil 10 minutes for rare, 13 minutes for medium and 15 minutes for well done, turning once after half the cooking time has elapsed. Sprinkle with salt and serve immediately.

4 beef loin top loin steaks, about 3/4 inch thick (1 1/2 to 2 pounds)
4 teaspoons peppercorns, coarsely crushed
1/2 cup dry red wine
Salt

4 servings

MARINATED BRANDY STEAK

With a sharp knife, remove excess fat and cut 5 or 6 1-inch slits in steak. Put cracked pepper in slits. Place steak on deep platter. In small bowl combine oil, vinegar, garlic, and onion salt. Spread mixture on steak and let stand 1 hour. Lightly brush grill grates with vegetable oil. Preheat grill on "Hi" for 5 minutes. Cook steak on grill according to time chart on page 2. Brush with marinade; turn. Grill until steak is done as desired. Place on a platter. In small saucepan warm brandy. Light with a match and pour over steak. When flame subsides slice and serve.

1 2-pound top round steak, 1/2 to 3/4 inch thick
1/2 teaspoon cracked black pepper
3 tablespoons vegetable oil
3 tablespoons cider vinegar
1 clove garlic, minced
1/2 teaspoon onion salt
1/4 cup brandy

4 to 6 servings

GARLIC BUTTER

Blend all ingredients in a food processor or by hand. Store in refrigerator or freezer and use to season vegetables, pasta, grilled meat, and for making garlic bread.

Note: Garlic butter will keep several days, tightly covered, in the refrigerator or freezer.

1/2 cup butter, softened
2 large cloves garlic, minced
2 tablespoons chopped parsley
1 tablespoon minced chives or scallions
1/2 teaspoon basil
1/4 teaspoon pepper
1/4 teaspoon salt (if unsalted butter is used)

1/2 cup

Grilled Hors d'Oeuvre (page 3)

MARINATED FLANK STEAK

1 1/2 pounds beef flank
          steak
   1/3 cup red wine vinegar
      1 tablespoon prepared
          horseradish
      1 tablespoon prepared
          mustard
      2 tablespoons vegetable
          oil
   1/4 teaspoon freshly
          ground pepper
      1 clove garlic, minced,
          or 2 teaspoons
          minced dry garlic

Trim surface fat from flank steak. Score steak surface in diamonds on both sides. In small bowl, combine vinegar, horseradish, mustard, oil, pepper, and garlic. Pour over steak in a shallow casserole or in a plastic bag. Cover and marinate steak 3 or 4 hours, turning occasionally. Lightly brush grill grates with vegetable oil. Preheat grill on "Hi" for 5 minutes. Place steak on hot grill and broil 10 minutes, turning after 5 minutes. (It is best to grill flank steak just until rare for best flavor and tenderness.) Slice steak thinly at an angle across the grain.

6 servings

LONDON BROIL
WITH BARBECUE SAUCE

      1 flank steak
          (1 1/2 pounds)
      6 slices bacon

Barbecue Sauce

   1/4 cup red wine vinegar
   1/4 cup catsup
      3 tablespoons salad oil
      1 teaspoon hot pepper
          sauce
   1/4 teaspoon garlic
          powder
   1/4 cup lemon juice
      1 teaspoon dry mustard
      2 tablespoons brown
          sugar
      2 tablespoons minced
          onion
1 1/2 teaspoons salt
   1/4 teaspoon cracked
          black pepper

Roll steak jelly-roll fashion and secure at 1-inch intervals with skewers. Cut steak crosswise into 6 slices about 1 inch thick. Combine all ingredients in barbecue sauce in saucepan with 1/4 cup water. Bring to boil; remove from heat. Marinate steak in barbecue sauce at least 5 hours or overnight. Refrigerate if marinating overnight. Just before grilling, remove steaks from sauce; reserve sauce. Wrap a bacon slice around each steak roll; secure with toothpicks or skewers. Lightly brush grill grates with vegetable oil. Preheat grill on "Hi" for 5 minutes. Place steak on grill; broil 10 minutes on each side or until tender and brown. Turn and baste frequently with reserved sauce.

6 servings

GRILLED HAMBURGERS

Hamburgers are a popular feature of grilled meals and picnics. You can make burgers with an outdoor taste on your kitchen grill. For basic hamburgers, form 2 pounds lean ground beef into eight 1/2-inch thick burgers. Lightly brush grill grates with vegetable oil. Preheat grill on "Hi" for 5 minutes; reduce temperature to "10". Grill burgers about 6 minutes per side for rare, 12 minutes for medium, 14 minutes for well done. When burgers are almost done, butter one side of hamburger buns or bread slices and grill, buttered side down, until lightly toasted. Place burgers on untoasted side of buns or bread and serve open or closed.

VARIATIONS:

Hamburgers Provençale

Divide Garlic Butter (page 5) into 16 pats of 1 tablespoon each. Place on waxed paper and freeze until very firm. Form meat into sixteen 1/4-inch thick oval patties. Top 8 patties with 2 tablespoons garlic butter. Place remaining patties on top of butter and pinch edges to seal. Grill burgers until done to taste. Serve with 8 thick slices French or Italian bread that have been buttered and grilled until lightly toasted.

Insiders' Cheeseburgers

Mix meat with 2 cups grated sharp Cheddar cheese, handling meat gently and briefly. Shape meat-cheese mixture into eight 1/2-inch thick burgers. Grill until done to taste. When burgers are almost done, grill 8 split, buttered hamburger buns until lightly toasted. Top buns with burgers, serve with sliced ripe tomatoes and sliced onions.

Hamburgers Lyonnaise

Blend meat with 1/4 cup finely minced onion, 1/2 cup heavy cream, and 1/2 teaspoon pepper, handling the meat as little as possible. Shape into eight 1/2-inch burgers. Grill burgers until done to taste. Grill 8 slices of buttered rye bread until lightly toasted. Place burgers on untoasted side of bread.

8 servings

MUSTARD-BASTED HAM

1/4 cup horseradish-flavored
         prepared mustard
1/4 cup pineapple juice
  1 tablespoon brown sugar
  1 slice fully cooked
         ham (1 1/2 to
         2 pounds)

Lightly brush grill grates with vegetable oil. Preheat grill on "Hi" for 5 minutes. Meanwhile mix mustard, juice, and brown sugar and heat gently in a small saucepan on the back of the grill. Grill ham slice about 8 minutes on each side, basting frequently with mustard sauce. Serve remaining sauce with hot ham.

6 servings

PORK CHOPS ORIENTAL

1/4 cup dry sherry
  2 tablespoons soy sauce
  2 tablespoons vegetable oil
1/2 teaspoon ginger
  4 pork loin chops,
         3/4 inch thick

Combine sherry, soy sauce, oil, and ginger in a shallow casserole. Add pork chops and spoon some of the mixture over them. Let stand 20 minutes. Lightly brush grill grates with vegetable oil. Preheat grill on "Hi" for 5 minutes. Place chops on grill and broil 20 minutes, turning once. Baste often with marinade. If desired, garnish with thin orange slices or sprigs of parsley. Serve with rice.

4 servings

COUNTRY BARBECUED RIBS

2 to 4 pounds country-style
         spareribs, cut in half
1/2 cup chopped onion
  2 teaspoons salt
1/2 teaspoon pepper

Barbecue Sauce

3/4 cup cider vinegar
1/2 teaspoon dry mustard
1/2 cup chopped onion
  1 tablespoon brown sugar
1/4 cup Worcestershire sauce
3/4 cup catsup
  1 tablespoon lemon juice
  1 clove garlic, crushed

Place spareribs spread with a mixture of onion, salt, and pepper on a rack in a 12×16×3-inch pan. Bake in convection oven on rack position 2 at 325° for 45 minutes to 1 hour. Meanwhile, combine all ingredients for Barbecue Sauce in a medium-size saucepan. Simmer for 1 hour, uncovered; stir occasionally. Sauce will be very thick. Remove ribs from roasting pan; discard accumulated fat. Lightly brush grill grates with vegetable oil. Preheat grill on "10" for 5 minutes. Place ribs on grill and brush generously with barbecue sauce. Grill 30 minutes, turning and brushing with sauce several times.

8 to 10 servings

FANCY FRANKS

Split frankfurters lengthwise but not completely through. Place desired filling in cut; wrap bacon around frank and secure with toothpick. Lightly brush grill grates with vegetable oil. Preheat grill on "Hi" for 5 minutes. Broil filled franks on grill for 12 to 15 minutes, turning frequently. Franks should be hot through and bacon well browned. To shorten cooking time, fry bacon in skillet for 2 minutes on each side and simmer franks in boiling water for 5 minutes before assembling stuffed franks.

Note: For a smaller number of franks, heat only half the grill

10 servings

10 frankfurters
   (about 1 pound)
10 slices bacon

Fillings

Pineapple spears
Cheddar cheese strips
Mandarin oranges,
   3 sections for
   each frank
Pickled mushrooms
Thin dill pickle spears
Sliced scallions
Apple slices

SAUSAGE HEROES

Lightly brush grill grates with vegetable oil. Preheat grill on "9" for 5 minutes. Add sausages and broil 20 minutes, turning frequently, until well done. Meanwhile, heat oil in a skillet. Add green peppers and onion and sauté, stirring often, until tender. Sprinkle with oregano and salt. Add tomato sauce and heat to simmering. Remove from heat and keep warm. Toast rolls over hot grill. Place sausages in rolls and spoon some of the green pepper sauce on each.

4 servings

1 pound mild (sweet)
   Italian sausage
3 tablespoons vegetable oil
2 medium-size green
   peppers, cut in
   long thin strips
1 large onion, cut in
   thin strips
1/2 teaspoon oregano
1/2 teaspoon salt
1 can (8 ounces)
   tomato sauce
4 long or 8 short
   Italian rolls

MIXED GRILL

Lightly brush grill grates with vegetable oil. Preheat grill on "Hi" for 5 minutes. Trim excess fat from chops. Wrap each chicken liver in a slice of bacon and secure with small skewer or wooden toothpick. Remove stems from mushrooms and reserve for another use. Place 2 teaspoons garlic butter in each mushroom cavity. Place lamb chops and tomato halves, cut side down, on grill and broil 4 minutes. Turn chops and add livers, sausages, and mushrooms, cavity side up. Grill 5 minutes, turning livers and sausages frequently. Don't turn mushrooms. About 2 minutes before chops are done, turn tomato, cut side up, and gently press charred surface with the back of a spoon to form a slight indentation. Add 1 teaspoon garlic butter and continue to grill until chops are done. Serve at once on heated plates.

4 servings

4 loin or rib lamb
   chops, 1 inch thick
8 chicken livers
8 slices bacon
8 large mushrooms
   Garlic Butter (page 5)
2 tomatoes, cut in half
8 breakfast sausages

GRILLED
MARINATED LAMB CHOPS

Combine oil, garlic, and mustard. Brush both sides of chops with mixture and set aside for 1 hour before grilling. Lightly brush grill grates with vegetable oil. Preheat grill on "Hi" for 5 minutes. Place chops on grill and broil until done to your taste, turning once. Serve hot.

6 servings

1/4 cup vegetable oil
1 clove garlic, mashed
1 tablespoon prepared
   mustard
6 loin lamb chops

Chops

3/4 inch thick	10 to 12 minutes each side
1 inch thick	14 to 16 minutes each side
1 1/2 inches thick	16 to 18 minutes each side

Chops should be juicy and slightly pink. Make a slit along the bone to test for doneness.

Mixed Grill

BUTTERFLIED LEG OF LAMB

1 4-pound boned leg of
     lamb, butterflied
     for grilling or
     broiling
2 large cloves garlic,
     thinly sliced
   Olive oil
1/2 teaspoon pepper
1 teaspoon rosemary,
     thyme, or oregano

Make tiny incisions all over meat with the point of a sharp knife and insert garlic slivers. Brush meaty side of lamb with olive oil and sprinkle both sides with pepper and herbs. Cover and refrigerate 30 to 60 minutes. Lightly brush the grill grates with vegetable oil. Preheat grill on "Hi" for 5 minutes. Place meat on grill and broil 15 to 18 minutes per side for medium rare. Increase cooking time 5 to 10 minutes for medium. When meat is done, remove it to a cutting board and let it stand 10 minutes before slicing. Cut meat across the grain into 1/4 to 1/2 inch thick slices. Serve with meat juices.

8 to 12 servings

SPICED CHICKEN BARBECUE

1 broiler-fryer chicken,
     cut into serving pieces
2 tablespoons butter
1 onion, diced
1/2 cup catsup
1/4 cup lemon juice
2 tablespoons brown sugar
2 tablespoons
     Worcestershire sauce
1 teaspoon dry mustard
1 teaspoon salt
1 teaspoon tarragon
1/2 teaspoon basil

Rinse chicken pieces and pat dry. Melt butter in large skillet. Sauté onion until transparent. Stir in 1/2 cup water and all remaining ingredients. Bring to a boil, reduce, and simmer 15 minutes stirring occasionally. Set aside. Lightly brush grill grates with vegetable oil. Preheat grill on "10" for 5 minutes. Place chicken pieces on grill and broil for 20 minutes, turning every 5 minutes. Brush chicken generously with barbecue sauce and continue grilling for 10 minutes. Turn chicken, brush with more sauce, and grill 5 to 10 minutes more.

4 servings

GRILLED LOBSTER TAILS

2 tablespoons butter or
     margarine
2 cloves garlic, minced
2 tablespoons olive oil
4 lobster tails,
     6 to 8 ounces each
1/2 cup butter or
     margarine, melted
1/4 cup lemon juice

Combine butter and garlic in skillet; sauté until tender. Stir in oil. Cut lobster tail down center. Loosen meat but leave meat in shell. Crack shell and turn back. Lightly brush grill grates with vegetable oil. Preheat grill on "8" for 5 minutes. Brush lobster tails with garlic mixture and grill 10 to 15 minutes on each side, brushing often with garlic mixture. Combine remaining butter and lemon juice. Serve with lobster tails.

4 servings

DILL GRILLED FISH STEAKS

1 1/2 cups mayonnaise
1/2 cup minced scallions
1/2 cup chopped dill or
    2 tablespoons dried
    dillweed
1 tablespoon lemon juice
1/2 teaspoon salt
1/2 teaspoon pepper
4 salmon or swordfish
    steaks, cut 1 inch
    thick

Combine all ingredients except fish in a bowl and blend. Set aside 1 cup of dill mayonnaise, cover, and refrigerate.   Lightly brush grill grates with vegetable oil. Preheat grill on "Hi" for 5 minutes. Spread one side of each fish steak with about 1 tablespoon of dill mayonnaise. Place steaks on grill, sauce side down, and broil 5 minutes for salmon, 6 1/2 minutes for swordfish. Spread top of each steak with 1 tablespoon of dill mayonnaise, turn with tongs, and grill 5 minutes longer for salmon, 6 1/2 minutes for swordfish. Serve with remaining dill mayonnaise.

4 servings

ROASTED CORN

6 ears fresh corn
Salt
Pepper
Butter

With husks: Turn back inner husk and remove silk. Close husks and soak in cold water for about 1 hour. Preheat grill on "Hi" for 5 minutes. Place corn on grill and turn frequently for 20 to 30 minutes. Serve with salt, pepper, and butter.

Without husks: Remove husks and silk. Place each ear on square of heavy-duty foil; add 1 tablespoon butter and wrap securely. Preheat grill on "Hi" for 5 minutes. Place corn on grill and turn frequently for 15 to 20 minutes.

6 servings

SWEET AND SOUR BEANS

1 package (9 ounces)
    frozen green beans,
    thawed
4 slices bacon, fried
    and crumbled
1/2 cup diced celery
1 tablespoon minced onion
1 tablespoon sugar
1 tablespoon cider vinegar
1/4 teaspoon salt
1/8 teaspoon pepper

Place beans, bacon, celery, and onion on 18×12-inch double thickness of heavy-duty foil; leave one side open. Combine remaining ingredients with 1 tablespoon water and pour into foil package; seal securely. Preheat grill on "Hi" for 5 minutes and place packet on half of grill while cooking meat on other half. Cook 20 to 25 minutes, or until beans are tender. Turn packet once.

4 servings

Dill Grilled Fish Steaks

JENN-AIR GRIDDLE

Imagine a cooking surface that is easy to clean, is large enough to cook a whole family meal at once, and that drains excess fat neatly into a jar for easy disposal. The Jenn-Air griddle does all of these. It is sure to be one of your favorite pieces of cooking equipment.

The griddle is excellent for cooking food you usually panfry: marinated meat, hamburger, stir-fry vegetables. Its size and acces-

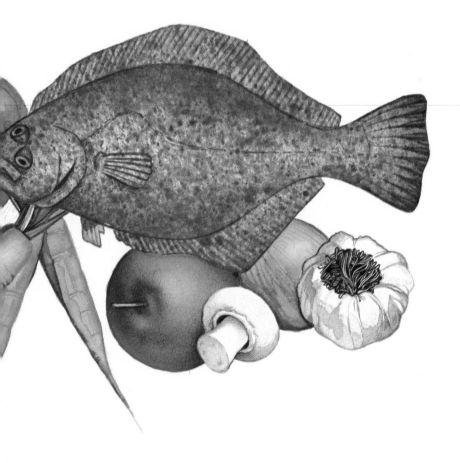

sibility (no skillet sides to hinder wielding the spatula!) make the griddle a natural for cooking pancakes, toasted sandwiches, and omelets.

For most recipes, the griddle should be *lightly* greased each time it is used. Metal spatulas can be used *with care* on the non-stick surface, but be careful not to scratch or scar it. A plastic spatula of the kind designed for use with non-stick skillets will give you more freedom; wooden spoons and spatulas are very good for stir-fry dishes. If you can use chopsticks, they work very well for moving and turning food on the griddle.

For best results, preheat griddle at the temperature specified in a recipe or on chart. Do *not* preheat or cook on the "Hi" setting. Be sure to turn the heat down after preheating if the recipe so directs.

The griddle can be cleaned like any other frying pan; be sure to remove any burned-on residue before using the griddle again. Clean with any soap or detergent. Remember to check the grease collection containers frequently. You may be surprised to find they fill up very quickly when a fatty meat like bacon is cooked on the griddle. Empty the containers when the grease is *cold*, of course.

Preheat 3 to 5 minutes at specified setting.

	Control Setting	Approximate Cooking Time (minutes)	
		First Side	Second Side
Sausage Patties	8	8	6
Bacon	8	3	1-2
Ham Slice	8	6	5-6
Hamburgers	7	6	5
Fish Sticks	6	5	3-4
Hot Dogs	8	5	5
Buns	8	3	
French Toast	9	3	2-3
Grilled Sandwiches	8	4	3
Pancakes	8	2-3	1-2
Eggs	6	3	(1)

STIR-FRY PEPPER STEAK

Wipe meat and cut into 1/4-inch strips. Cut strips into 3-inch lengths. Toss in a large bowl with oregano, garlic powder, soy sauce, pepper, and dry sherry. Let stand at least 10 minutes. When ready to cook, heat griddle on "8" for 3 to 5 minutes. Grease griddle lightly with vegetable oil (add some more oil as needed). Put green pepper strips, mushrooms, and scallions on the griddle; stir and turn so that all sides cook evenly, about 5 minutes. Add steak strips to the griddle; fry about 3 minutes, stirring constantly so that all sides cook. When the steak has just lost its pink color, pour any marinade left over the meat and vegetables (if none is left, use a little more sherry, about 1 tablespoon). Cook another minute and serve at once. Plain white rice is very good with all stir-fry dishes. Pass more soy sauce at the table.

Note: Meat is easier to slice in thin, even slices if it is partially frozen.

6 servings

1 1/2	pounds round steak
1/2	teaspoon oregano
1/2	teaspoon garlic powder
3	tablespoons soy sauce
1/2	teaspoon pepper
1/2	cup dry sherry
3	tablespoons vegetable oil
2	large green peppers, seeded and cut into 1/4-inch strips
1	cup sliced mushrooms
3	scallions cut diagonally into 1-inch slices

BEEF AND CHEDDAR BURGERS

In a bowl combine the meat, cheese, chili sauce, onion, salt, and pepper and blend thoroughly. Butter one side of each bread slice; shape meat mixture into 6 patties; place patties on unbuttered sides of half the slices. Close the sandwiches with the remaining bread, buttered sides up. Heat the griddle on "8" for 3 to 5 minutes. Fry the sandwiches 4 minutes per side until bread is golden and filling is cooked medium rare. Cut sandwiches in half to serve. Garnish with pickles and olives.

6 servings

1	pound lean ground beef
1	cup grated sharp Cheddar cheese
2	tablespoons chili sauce or catsup
2	tablespoons minced onion
1/2	teaspoon salt
1/4	teaspoon pepper
12	slices firm white bread Butter, softened Pickles (optional) Olives (optional)

JAPANESE TERIYAKI STIR-FRY

1/3 cup soy sauce
1/3 cup dry sherry
  1 tablespoon sugar
  2 teaspoons minced fresh
       gingerroot or 1/2 teaspoon
       ground ginger
  1 large clove garlic, minced
  1 pound lean boneless
       beef (flank or top round)
1/2 pound mushrooms,
       thinly sliced
  1 large onion, thinly
       sliced and
       separated into rings
1/2 pound fresh bean sprouts
  2 tablespoons cold
       butter or margarine

Combine the soy sauce, sherry, sugar, ginger, and garlic in a glass bowl and mix until sugar dissolves. Cut meat across the grain into very thin slices. Add to marinade, cover and refrigerate 1 hour or longer. When ready to serve preheat griddle 5 minutes on "10." Grease griddle lightly with vegetable oil. Drain meat and stir-fry 40 to 60 seconds. Remove meat to a plate and keep warm. Mound vegetables on griddle and place butter in center of vegetables. Stir-fry 2 to 3 minutes until vegetables are hot but remain crisp. Return meat to griddle and toss quickly with vegetables. Serve with rice.

4 to 6 servings

Nice to know: Using these basic proportions and techniques, you can vary the ingredients and invent an endless variety of stir-fry dishes.

LIVER AND ONIONS

1 1/2 pounds calves' liver,
         sliced very thin
  1/2 cup wheat germ
    2 tablespoons
         vegetable oil
    6 scallions,
         thinly sliced
    1 tablespoon butter
    2 tablespoons
         dry sherry

Cut the liver into 2×2-inch pieces. Heat the griddle for 5 minutes on "9". Roll liver slices in wheat germ. Grease griddle generously with vegetable oil and place coated pieces of liver on griddle. Reduce heat to "6" and watch liver carefully; turn as soon as coating is lightly browned. When the liver is turned, add the butter to one side of the griddle and put the onions in it to cook lightly. Stir and turn so that onions cook evenly, about 4 minutes. Pour sherry over meat and onions, stir to mix well and heat through. Serve at once.

6 servings

Nice to know: An interesting variation of this dish is mushrooms and sweet sherry or vermouth instead of scallions and dry sherry.

Japanese Teriyaki Stir-Fry

CHICKEN LIVERS WITH MUSHROOMS AND SOUR CREAM

1 1/2 pounds chicken livers
3 tablespoons butter
8 ounces mushrooms, sliced
1 cup dairy sour cream
1 tablespoon dry sherry
1/2 teaspoon salt
1 tablespoon minced parsley or
1 teaspoon dry parsley

Pat livers dry and cut them in half, removing any membranes. Heat the griddle for 3 minutes on "8." Melt butter on griddle and fry mushrooms and livers until the livers are lightly browned on both sides, about 3 to 5 minutes in all. Do not overcook. Remove to warm serving dish. Combine sour cream and sherry and heat gently. Pour over livers and mushrooms; add salt and mix. Sprinkle with parsley. Serve at once. Rice or a wheat pilaf would be especially good with this dish.

6 servings

SOLE CHIFFON

6 baby sole or flounder, about 3 pounds in all, or 2 pounds sole or flounder fillets, thawed if frozen
2 egg whites, lightly beaten
1 cup all-purpose flour
1 teaspoon salt
Lemon wedges
Parsley sprigs

If you have whole baby sole or flounder, wash it under cold running water, dry with paper towels, and dip it into egg whites before dredging in flour and salt mixed together. Heat the griddle on "8" for 3 to 5 minutes. Grease generously with butter and fry fish about 3 minutes on each side starting with the bottom of the fish (the dark side). Do not overcook the fish as it is very delicate. If you are using fillets, select pieces of fish that are fairly uniform in thickness. Save very thin ends for a fish chowder. Prepare and fry as for whole fish but be very careful about the cooking time. If the fish overcooks it will toughen and the flavor will not be as delicate. Serve as soon as it's done with lemon wedges and parsley for garnish.

6 servings

PUFFY OMELETS

Beat egg whites with salt until they form soft, moist peaks. Beat egg yolks until thoroughly mixed. Add pepper and hot pepper sauce. Heat griddle on "9" for 5 minutes. Melt butter and spread evenly on griddle. Fold egg yolks carefully into beaten egg whites; for each omelet, drop a scant cup of egg mixture onto the greased griddle leaving room between them. Cook about 3 minutes, or until bottoms of omelets are lightly browned. Reduce heat to "3" and turn omelets. Cook another 3 to 4 minutes, until bottoms are browned and omelets are fairly firm.

8 eggs, separated
1/2 teaspoon salt
1/2 teaspoon pepper
Dash hot pepper sauce
3 tablespoons butter or margarine

VARIATIONS:

Omelet Russe

Make two large omelets instead of 4 individual ones. As soon as egg mixture is on the griddle, deeply score the omelets across their diameters. Place 2 tablespoons red caviar and 2 tablespoons dairy sour cream along each depression. When the omelets are barely browned on the bottom, fold each one in half. Cook 2 minutes more, then turn to other side and cook another 2 minutes. Serve with more sour cream.

Garden Omelets

Add 1 cup cooked chopped vegetables to eggs before cooking. Some excellent combinations are: 1/2 cup spinach and 1/2 cup sautéed onion; broccoli and onion; and summer squash and parsley. Sprinkle finished omelets with grated sharp cheese.

4 servings

GRIDDLE OMELETS

2 eggs, very lightly
   beaten
1 teaspoon cold water
   Dash salt
   Dash pepper
1 tablespoon butter or
   margarine

Mix eggs, water, salt, and pepper. Heat griddle on "8" for 3 to 5 minutes. Melt butter and spread evenly over griddle. Pour egg mixture onto griddle. Lift edges so that uncooked egg runs onto griddle surface. When the bottom of the omelet is lightly browned, lift and roll it into thirds. Cooking should take only about 3 minutes; be sure not to overcook. The eggs will continue to cook after they are served on a warmed plate.

VARIATION:

Dessert Omelets

Follow recipe for Griddle Omelets but omit pepper. Before rolling, place 2 tablespoons jelly on top of omelet. Sprinkle with powdered sugar before serving.

1 serving

TORTILLA D'ESPAÑA (VEGETABLE OMELETS)

1 medium-size zucchini
2 large carrots
1 green pepper, cored
   and seeded
1 large tomato
1/2 cup thinly sliced
   scallions
3 eggs
2 large cloves garlic,
   minced
1/2 cup all-purpose flour
1 teaspoon baking
   powder
1 teaspoon salt
   Vegetable oil
   Dairy sour cream
   Taco sauce

Grate the zucchini and carrots into a bowl. Mince the pepper and tomato and add to bowl with the scallions. Toss vegetables to blend. In a separate bowl beat the eggs with the garlic. Stir in the flour, baking powder and salt and blend well. Add egg mixture to vegetables and blend. Heat griddle on "8" for 3 to 5 minutes. Lightly grease griddle with vegetable oil and drop batter onto griddle using about 1/4 cup for each pancake. Flatten pancakes with the back of a spatula as they cook. Cook about 2 minutes per side, until brown and crisp around the edges. Serve pancakes hot with sour cream and taco sauce.

6 servings

GRIDDLE POTATO CHIPS

Peel potatoes and slice crosswise into 1/8-inch slices. Place in a large bowl of iced water and let stand at least 20 minutes. When ready to cook, drain potatoes and carefully dry each slice. Heat the griddle on "9" for 5 minutes. Grease very generously with oil (add more as needed). Place potato slices in a single layer on the griddle; fry about 5 minutes, or until bottom side is quite brown. Turn potatoes carefully; reduce heat to "8." Continue frying until other side is done. Drain on paper towels and sprinkle with salt. Serve hot.

Note: If all the potato slices will not go on the griddle in a single layer at once, make two batches. It is important that the potato chips have enough room to cook without touching each other.

6 servings

6 medium-size
   all-purpose potatoes
1/2 cup vegetable oil
   Salt

SPINACH PIE SANDWICHES

Squeeze spinach to remove excess moisture. Melt butter in a large skillet. Add onion and spinach and sauté 5 minutes until onion is soft, and moisture from spinach has evaporated. Remove pan from heat and stir in cottage cheese, Parmesan cheese, egg, dillweed, salt, and pepper. Butter one side of each bread slice, and place a slice of cheese on the unbuttered side of 6 of the slices. Divide the spinach filling among the cheese-topped bread slices and close sandwiches with the remaining bread, buttered sides up. Heat griddle on "8" for 5 minutes. Toast sandwiches about 3 minutes per side until bread is golden brown and filling is hot. Cut sandwiches in half before serving. Garnish with cherry tomatoes and oil-cured olives.

6 servings

2 packages (10 ounces)
   chopped frozen
   spinach, thawed
1/4 cup butter or
   margarine
1/2 cup diced onion
2 cups cottage cheese
1 cup grated Parmesan
   cheese
1 egg
1 teaspoon dillweed
1/2 teaspoon salt
1/4 teaspoon pepper
   Butter or margarine,
   softened
12 slices whole wheat
   bread
6 slices Muenster,
   Swiss or provolone
   cheese
   Cherry tomatoes
   Oil-cured olives

GRIDDLE TACOS

Homemade or ready-made corn or flour tortillas. *Suggested fillings:* chili con carne, cooked sausage, refried beans, grated sharp cheese, shredded lettuce, chopped tomatoes, diced onion, mashed avocado or guacamole, dairy sour cream

Tortillas become tacos when they are heated and stuffed with any kind of appropriate filling. The large griddle surface is perfect for heating homemade or ready-made tortillas. If frozen tortillas are used, remove them from the package, brush off ice crystals, and spread them out in a single layer. They will thaw in about 5 minutes. If tortillas seem dry around the edges, sprinkle lightly with water before heating. Heat griddle on "8" for 3 to 5 minutes. Grease griddle lightly with vegetable oil. Place tortillas on griddle in a single layer and cook 30 to 60 seconds, turning often, until they are soft and hot. Fill with any of the suggested fillings or combination of fillings, fold or roll, and serve immediately. If desired, tortillas can be heated on griddle, then transferred to a covered casserole and kept warm in a 200° oven until all tortillas are heated.

FRIED GREEN TOMATOES

Wash and dry unpeeled tomatoes. Cut in 3/8- to 1/2-inch slices. Spread cornmeal, salt, and pepper in a shallow plate and mix well. Dip the tomato slices in meal; coat well on both sides. Heat the griddle for 3 minutes on "9." Grease generously with butter (add more as needed). Place coated tomato slices, not touching, on griddle. Reduce heat to "8"; fry tomatoes until bottom side is golden brown, about 5 minutes. Turn and brown other side. Drain, if necessary, briefly on brown paper before serving hot.

Note: Many vegetables may be fried on the griddle. Summer squash, eggplant, and whole green beans would be very good. Fry each vegetable until coating is brown and vegetable crisp-tender.

6 servings

2 large firm green tomatoes
3/4 cup cornmeal
1 teaspoon salt
1/2 teaspoon pepper
6 tablespoons butter or margarine

Griddle Tacos

OLD-FASHIONED POTATO PANCAKES

Combine potatoes and onion in a large bowl. Add egg and matzoh meal and stir to blend. Stir in salt and pepper. Mixture should be thick enough to mound when dropped onto griddle. Add more matzoh meal if needed. Heat griddle on "8" for 3 to 5 minutes. Grease generously with oil and drop batter by scant 1/4-cup measures onto griddle. Cook about 2 minutes per side until pancakes are well browned on each side. Serve with apple sauce and sour cream or plain yogurt as a side dish or light meal.

about 24 pancakes

Nice to know: Drop about 1 tablespoon of batter on hot griddle to make miniature pancakes, wonderful as appetizers. Cooked pancakes can be wrapped and frozen, available to use when unexpected company appears. Just place frozen pancakes on baking sheet and heat 10 to 15 minutes in a 350° oven.

6 cups grated
    potato (about 6
    medium-size
    all-purpose
    potatoes)
1 large onion, grated
1 egg
1/2 cup matzoh meal or
    cracker crumbs
1/2 teaspoon pepper
1 teaspoon salt
    Vegetable oil

DOUBLE CORN PANCAKES

In a large bowl combine and mix dry ingredients well. Add the eggs, milk and butter and stir to blend. Stir in the corn. Heat griddle on "8" for 3 to 5 minutes. Grease griddle lightly with vegetable oil. Drop batter by scant 1/4-cup measures on griddle and cook pancakes approximately 1½ minutes, or until lightly browned on the first side, and 1 minute on the second. Serve with butter and syrup or honey or, for a light supper, topped with chili and grated Cheddar cheese.

16 4-inch pancakes

1 cup all-purpose flour
1 cup yellow or white
    cornmeal
4 teaspoons baking
    powder
2 tablespoons sugar
1 1/2 teaspoons salt
2 eggs
1 1/4 cups milk
1/4 cup melted butter
    or cooking oil
1 package (10 ounces)
    frozen corn, thawed,
    or 1 cup cooked or
    canned corn, drained

Old-Fashioned Potato Pancakes
Basic Pancakes (page 30)
Yogurt and Cottage Cheese Pancakes (page 31)
Double Corn Pancakes

SWISS CHEESE PANCAKES

1/2   cup whole wheat
      or white
      all-purpose flour
1   cup dairy sour cream
4   eggs
1   teaspoon salt
1/4   teaspoon nutmeg
2   cups grated Swiss
      cheese
      Vegetable oil

Combine flour and sour cream and mix. Blend in the eggs, and when smooth, add salt, nutmeg, and then cheese. Heat griddle on "8" for 3 to 5 minutes. Grease lightly with oil and, using about 2 tablespoons per pancake, drop batter onto hot griddle. Cook pancakes about 2 minutes per side. Serve with apple butter or apple sauce and sour cream. They are also delicious with sour cream and thinly sliced scallions.

24 3-inch pancakes

BASIC PANCAKES
OR GRIDDLECAKES

1 1/2   cups sifted
        all-purpose flour
1   teaspoon salt
2   teaspoons baking
      powder
1   tablespoon sugar
1   cup milk or water
1   egg
2   tablespoons melted
      butter or margarine

Combine dry ingredients in a bowl. Add the remaining ingredients and beat with a fork or whisk until well blended. Heat griddle 3 to 5 minutes on "8." Drop batter by 1/4 cup measures onto the lightly oiled griddle and cook about 1 1/2 minutes, until tiny bubbles cover the top of each pancake. Turn and cook 1 minute longer, or until lightly browned. Add more oil to grease griddle as necessary. Cooked pancakes can be kept in a 200° oven while the remainder bake. They are, of course, best eaten right from the griddle. Serve with warm syrup or honey and sweet butter.

about 12 pancakes

VARIATIONS:

Apple Pancakes

Add 1/4 teaspoon cinnamon with dry ingredients in basic recipe. Stir 1 cup finely chopped, peeled, and cored apples into batter just before baking.

Blueberry Pancakes

Add 1/2 cup sweetened fresh blueberries or still frozen blueberries to batter just before baking.

YOGURT AND COTTAGE CHEESE PANCAKES

Combine cottage cheese, yogurt, and egg yolks in a bowl and blend. Stir in flour, lemon peel, sugar, salt, and butter and mix well. Beat egg whites until soft peaks form and fold into batter. Heat griddle on "8" for 3 to 5 minutes. Using about 3 table-spoons of batter for each pancake, drop batter onto hot griddle and cook about 1 1/2 to 2 minutes per side or until lightly browned. Serve with stewed fruits or berries and yogurt or sour cream.

about 24 pancakes

1 cup cottage cheese
1 cup plain yogurt or dairy sour cream
4 eggs, separated
1 cup all-purpose flour
1 teaspoon finely grated lemon peel
1 tablespoon sugar
1 teaspoon salt
4 tablespoons melted butter or cooking oil

TOASTED SANDWICHES

Butter one side of each bread slice. Arrange half the slices, buttered side down, on a plate. Spread each slice of bread with a fourth of the fillings. Close sandwiches with remaining bread slices, buttered sides up. Press firmly to enclose fillings. Heat griddle on "8" for 3 to 5 minutes. Place sandwiches on griddle and cook 2 to 3 minutes per side. Cut in half and serve. Many combinations of fillings are good; you may enjoy:

4 servings

8 slices firm white bread
Butter, softened
About 1/2 cup fillings

Wisconsin Apple Butter Sandwiches

Use 1 package (8 slices) sharp Cheddar cheese slices and 1/2 cup apple butter.

QUICK GRIDDLE BISCUITS

Place biscuit mix and raisins in a bowl and toss raisins until they are well coated with mix. Stir in milk just until dry ingredients are well moistened. Heat griddle on "6" for 3 to 5 minutes. Lightly grease griddle with oil and drop batter onto griddle using about 1 tablespoon for each biscuit. Bake biscuits 4 minutes per side until crisp and brown. Split biscuits, butter and serve immediately. These griddle biscuits are best when eaten hot.

about 12 biscuits

2 cups biscuit baking mix
1/2 cup raisins or currants (optional)
3/4 cup milk
Vegetable oil

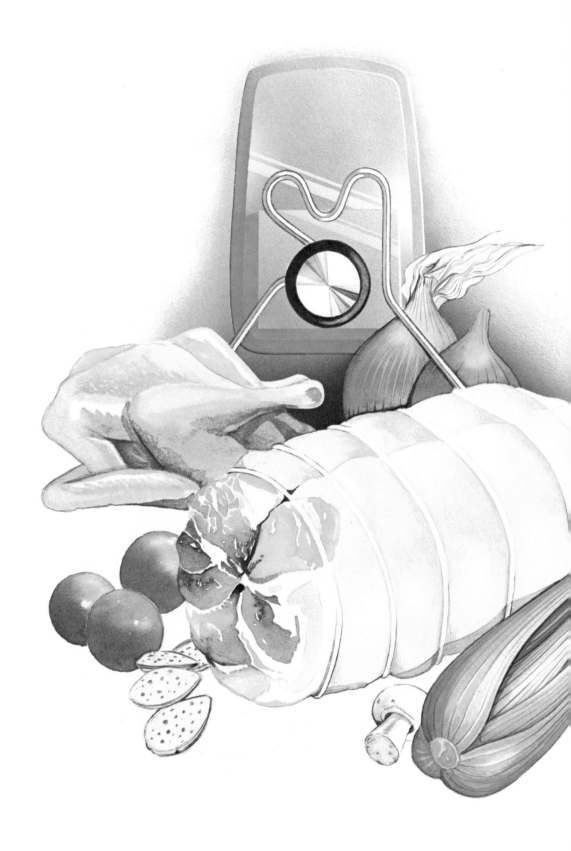

JENN-AIR ROTISSERIE

Spit roasting is an exciting way to prepare meat, but it used to require a pit dug outdoors and willing (and strong) hands to turn the spit for a long time. Now Jenn-Air's rotisserie attachment makes open-air spit roasting easy. The integral exhaust system means that the kitchen will not get hot or smoky while the meat is getting its outdoor grilled flavor. Best of all, while meat is roasting, it needs very little attention.

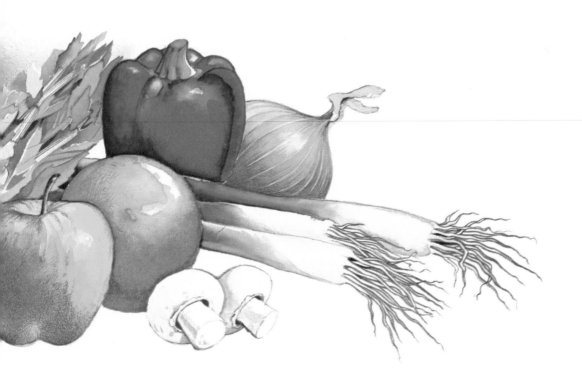

The meat must be well balanced and centered on the spit. Spear the meat and secure it with the 2 meat probes. Check the balance by holding the spit rod across your palms; if the spit and the meat do not rotate easily and evenly, remove the probes and spit and try again.

Poultry should be trussed with the legs and wings held close to the body (not tucked behind as one would usually do for oven roasting). Tie the bird at 1½-inch intervals to make sure it stays in a compact bundle. Insert the spit just above the tail and bring it out just above the wishbone. Rolled roasts and other large pieces of boneless meat should also be tied firmly at intervals with heavy string. A bone-in cut need not be tied, but it may be hard to balance. It is usually most successful to spit through bone-in meat on the diagonal.

Use the lower spit position for roasting most meat. The times given are for the lower position; if your cut of meat is larger than can be accommodated in the lower position, use the higher rotisserie position and adjust cooking time accordingly. Don't crowd the spit; there should be 2½ inches free at each end because the heating element does not run the entire length of the spit.

The most accurate way to determine when rotisseried meat is done to your taste is to use a meat thermometer. Turn off heat and the rotisserie motor; insert thermometer into the thickest part of the meat. Be certain that the thermometer bulb does not touch bone, fat, or the spit itself.

Differences in voltage in different areas (and even at different times of the day in the same area) may affect the time needed to roast meat on the rotisserie. Rely on the meat thermometer for accurate estimation of doneness. Since the meat will continue to cook after it has been removed from the heat, it is advisable to take meat that is to be served rare or medium off the rotisserie when the meat thermometer registers 5 to 10 degrees below the temperature specified. Let the meat stand 10 to 15 minutes before carving. It will be easier to carve and lose less juice if it is allowed to rest before being carved.

	Setting	Time (minutes)	Meat Thermometer Temp.
Beef Roast (Well Done)	HI	45 per lb.	160°
Pork Loin Roast	10	45 per lb.	170°
Leg of Lamb	HI	45 per lb.	170°
Chicken, Medium	HI	120 (total)	185°
Cornish Game Hen	HI	60 (total)	185°

(1) Above times are approximate (with grates removed).

(2) Preheating is optional.

(3) Roasts of approximately 3 to 3½ lbs. are the most suitable for rotissing.

(4) Above times based on using the low position.

BEEF STUFFED WITH MUSHROOMS

Melt butter in a large skillet. Add mushrooms, scallions, salt, lemon juice, and pepper. Sauté over very low heat until liquid from the mushrooms evaporates and the mixture turns very dark brown, about 30 minutes. While mushrooms cook, wipe meat dry. Place between sheets of waxed paper and flatten with mallet or rolling pin so that the meat is about 1/2 inch thick and very flat. Spread cooked mushroom mixture evenly over meat and roll up tightly starting with the long side. Tie every 1 1/2 inches. Preheat grill element (grates removed), for 5 minutes on "Hi." Thread rolled beef on spit and secure with meat probes. Roast in low position until internal temperature of meat reaches 140°, about 45 minutes. Let rest 5 minutes, remove strings, then slice diagonally and serve hot.

1/4 cup butter
1 pound mushrooms, chopped
2 scallions, white parts only, finely chopped
1/2 teaspoon salt
1 teaspoon lemon juice
Dash pepper
3 pounds round steak or boneless lean chuck shoulder steak

6 to 8 servings

GLAZED SMOKED PORK SHOULDER ROLL

Remove casing from meat and tie tightly every 1 1/2 inches with string. Insert spit through center of meat lengthwise, carefully balancing meat, and secure with 2 meat probes. Preheat grill element (grates removed), on "Hi" for 5 minutes. Reduce heat to "10" and roast meat in low position. Combine remaining ingredients and brush over meat after 1 hour of roasting, then baste frequently. If your pork roll is fully cooked, roast until internal temperature reaches 150°, about 2 to 2 1/2 hours. If the meat is smoked but not precooked, roast until internal temperature reaches 170°, about 3 hours. Serve thinly sliced, hot or cold. Hot English-style mustard is very good with this pork.

1 smoked boneless pork shoulder roll (butt), (about 3 pounds)
1/4 cup honey
2 tablespoons lemon juice
1 teaspoon soy sauce
1 tablespoon vegetable oil
1/8 teaspoon ground clove

Note: Read labels and wrappers on pork products carefully to find out whether meat is fully cooked or only smoked.

6 servings

PORK BUTT
WITH MUSTARD SAUCE

Remove wrapping from meat; tie with string every 1 1/2 inches. Arrange meat on spit, balancing very carefully. Preheat grill element (grates removed), on "Hi" for 5 minutes, then reduce heat to "10." Roast pork in low position until internal temperature reaches 150° for fully cooked products (about 2 hours) and to 170° for smoked but not precooked meat (about 3 hours). While meat roasts, combine mustard, flour, sugar, and salt in a 1-quart saucepan; add 2/3 cup water; stir to blend flour evenly. Cook on medium heat, stirring occasionally, until mixture thickens. Simmer 5 minutes. Remove from heat; stir in vinegar and sour cream. Slice meat and serve with warm mustard sauce.

1 smoked boneless pork
  shoulder roll
  (butt), (about
  3 pounds)
2 to 3 tablespoons dry
  mustard
2 tablespoons
  all-purpose flour
3 tablespoons sugar
1/2 teaspoon salt
1 tablespoon cider
  vinegar
2 tablespoons dairy
  sour cream

6 to 8 servings

APPLE BARBECUED PORK LOIN

Arrange meat on spit so that it is well balanced. Fasten securely with 2 meat probes. Preheat grill element (grates removed), on "Hi" for 5 minutes. Reduce heat to "10" and roast meat in low position. Mix remaining ingredients for basting and simmer together for 5 minutes. When roast is hot, baste frequently (a pastry brush is most efficient). Roast and baste for 2 1/2 to 3 hours, or until internal temperature reaches 170°. Slice thin and serve with more applesauce.

1 boneless rolled pork
  loin (3 to 4 pounds)
1/2 cup red wine vinegar
1 clove garlic, crushed
1/4 teaspoon rosemary
3/4 cup catsup
1 teaspoon salt
1/2 teaspoon pepper
2 teaspoons
  Worcestershire sauce
1/4 cup sugar
1/2 cup applesauce

6 to 8 servings

Apple Barbecued Pork Loin

SPARERIBS ON A SPIT

3 pounds pork spareribs,
  cut in half
  crosswise
1/2 cup chicken stock or
  bouillon
1/4 cup honey
1/4 cup catsup
1/4 cup soy sauce
  2 cloves garlic, minced

Place spareribs in a large pot of boiling water; boil 5 minutes; drain. Combine remaining ingredients. Pour over spareribs, cover, and refrigerate 3 to 4 hours, turning occasionally. Drain. Preheat grill element (grates removed), on "Hi" for 5 minutes. Weave spareribs onto spit, accordion fashion. Roast in low position about 60 minutes, basting occasionally with marinade. Remove from spit, cut into serving-size pieces, and serve hot.

2 to 3 servings

ORANGE GLAZED
CANADIAN BACON

1 whole Canadian bacon
  (2 to 2 1/2 pounds)
2 tablespoons frozen
  orange juice concentrate,
  thawed
1/4 cup honey
1 teaspoon vegetable oil
1 teaspoon soy sauce

Remove casing from bacon. Tie tightly with string at 1-inch intervals. Balance meat evenly on spit and fasten securely with 2 meat probes. Preheat grill element (grates removed), on "Hi" for 5 minutes. Mix all remaining ingredients for glaze. Roast bacon in low position 1 hour and 30 minutes, or until internal temperature reaches 170°. After 1 hour baste bacon frequently with glaze mixture.

8 to 10 servings

Nice to know: Substitute maple syrup for orange juice for a breakfast bacon treat.

*Spareribs on a Spit
Roasted Corn (page 14)*

STUFFED CORNISH HENS

4 tablespoons butter or
    margarine, divided
1/3 cup raisins
1/4 cup chopped pecans
1/4 cup chopped celery
2 tablespoons chopped
    onion
1/4 teaspoon rosemary
3/4 cup day-old bread cubes
1/4 teaspoon poultry
    seasoning
Salt and pepper
2 Cornish hens (about
    1 to 1 1/4 pounds each)
Paprika

Melt 2 tablespoons of the butter in a small skillet. Add raisins, pecans, celery, onion, and rosemary; cook until onion and celery are softened. Stir in bread cubes, 1/4 cup water, poultry seasoning, salt, and pepper. Divide stuffing between Cornish hens. Secure openings and tie hens firmly. Preheat grill element (grates removed), on "Hi" for 5 minutes. Arrange hens on spit in low position. Sprinkle hens with paprika and brush with remaining 2 tablespoons of butter, melted. Cook about 1 to 1 1/2 hours, or until hens are tender, browned, and the juice runs clear when the thigh is pricked.

Note: Use hen giblets to make stock. It makes excellent gravy thickened slightly with flour, or it may be used as the base for other sauces or soups.

2 servings

CHICKEN BURGUNDY

1 roasting chicken
    (about 4 pounds)
1/2 cup vegetable oil
1/2 cup Burgundy or other
    dry red wine
1 teaspoon marjoram
1 teaspoon minced
    parsley
1 teaspoon salt
1/4 teaspoon pepper

Wash and dry chicken. Combine all remaining ingredients. Pour marinade over chicken in deep bowl; cover and refrigerate for several hours; turn once or twice. Drain chicken and reserve marinade. Dry chicken thoroughly and tie wings and legs close to body. Carefully balance the chicken on spit and secure with meat probes. Preheat grill element (grates removed) 5 minutes on "Hi." Roast chicken in low position until internal breast temperature reaches 185°, about 1 hour and 45 minutes. Baste with marinade every 15 to 20 minutes.

4 to 6 servings

SPIT-BARBECUED
TURKEY BREAST

Have butcher bone turkey breast, roll it as neatly as possible with the skin on the outside, and tie it with string. Dry the outside of the roast and balance carefully on spit. Secure with 2 meat probes. Combine ingredients for Barbecue Sauce with 1 cup water in a small saucepan and bring to a boil over high heat, stirring constantly. Reduce temperature and simmer, covered, for 20 minutes. While sauce simmers, preheat grill element (grates removed), on "Hi" for 5 minutes. Roast turkey breast in low position; begin basting after 20 minutes and baste frequently thereafter. Roast until internal temperature reaches 185°, about 3 hours. Serve sliced, hot or cold.

Note: This recipe makes a good basic Barbecue Sauce.

12 to 15 servings

1 turkey breast
    (8 to 10 pounds)

Barbecue Sauce

1 cup catsup
2 tablespoons lemon
    juice
1/4 cup Worcestershire
    sauce
3 tablespoons brown
    sugar
1 teaspoon chili powder
1/2 teaspoon salt

JENN-AIR SHISH KEBAB ACCESSORY

Shish kebabs make any meal festive. The Jenn-Air shish kebab accessory makes preparation easy. The recipes in this section are for some classic kebabs. No doubt you will find other exciting combinations.

Lean lamb is the traditional meat for skewer cooking, but chunks of beef, pork, poultry, seafood, and pre-cooked meat are also very good. Shish kebabs offer one of the best ways to use leftover meat; just cut it up and flavor and decorate it to make a whole new meal. Vegetables

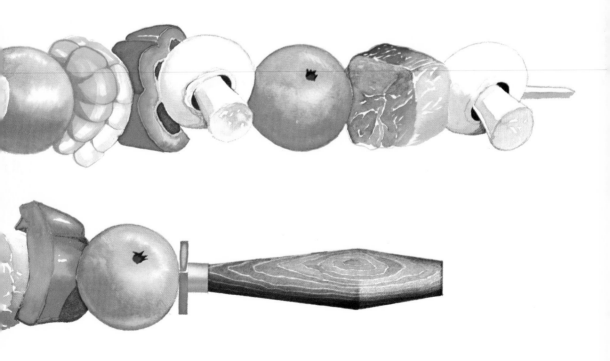

and fruit used in kebabs should be firm and of the kind that will hold together during cooking. Squares of red or green bell peppers, mushroom caps, and cherry tomatoes work well. Small whole onions may cook in the time needed to cook the meat, or they can be parboiled for about 5 minutes before broiling. Small new potatoes, chunks of carrots, cubes of squash and eggplant can be parboiled before being used in shish kebabs. Fresh pineapple chunks also work well. Canned pineapple chunks can be used for kebabs that cook up to about 15 minutes. Many foods are easier to insert on skewers if you pierce them with a poultry pin before inserting the skewer.

The delicate flavor the broiling imparts is especially good for appetizers and snacks. Marinate 1-inch chunks of frankfurters in spicy catsup and cook on skewers. Adults and children alike will ask for more. For an inexpensive treat, try chicken wings basted with butter and lemon juice. And children are sure to enjoy wonderful, if messy, toasted marshmallows you make for them on the skewers.

Meat usually should be marinated to provide extra tenderness and flavor. Use the marinade to brush over the kebabs as they broil. The flavor of chicken and fish will be enhanced by plain melted butter. Brush the kebabs rather than basting in order to prevent drippings from falling into the heating element.

It is important to balance the skewers well. Make sure meat and vegetables are firmly skewered through the center and that they turn as the skewer turns. Toothpicks are helpful for securing soft meat.

The two skewers in the middle positions receive more heat than the outside skewers. Use the center positions for the ingredients that take the longest time to cook. Or move the skewers halfway through the cooking time.

Don't crowd the skewers; there should be 2½ inches free at each end of each skewer because the heating element does not run the entire length of the spit. There should also be room for heat to circulate freely around each piece of food. The best way to check the degree of doneness of the kebab is to take a cube of meat off the skewer and cut into it. Voltage differences may make cooking times slightly different at various times; check meat to be sure it is cooked properly. Avoid overcooking skewered meat; it is usually most tender and tasty when cooked rare or medium.

BEEF KEBABS

Combine wine, soy sauce, olive oil, and garlic; add beef cubes and toss to coat well. Cover and refrigerate at least 2 hours or overnight. In small saucepan, melt butter; add flour and stir until smooth. Slowly add consommé and bring to a boil; reduce heat and simmer 10 minutes. Stir in tomato paste and simmer 5 minutes. Reserve for sauce. Peel new potatoes and place in boiling, salted water. Boil for 10 minutes; drain. Preheat grill element (grates removed), on "Hi" for 3 to 5 minutes. Remove beef from marinade and skewer on 2 skewers. Place in center positions. Broil 20 minutes (rare), 25 minutes (medium), or 30 minutes (well-done). Skewer potatoes, cherry tomatoes and green peppers; place on outside positions. Broil during last 15 minutes. Remove to serving platter. Reheat sauce and serve with meat and vegetables.

1 cup dry red wine
1/2 cup soy sauce
1/2 cup olive oil
1 clove garlic, crushed
2 pounds top round, cut into 1 1/2-inch cubes
2 tablespoons butter or margarine
2 tablespoons all-purpose flour
1 can (10 1/2 ounces) beef consommé, undiluted
1 tablespoon tomato paste
8 new potatoes
8 cherry tomatoes
2 green peppers, cut into 1-inch squares

VARIATION:

In place of potatoes, cut very small, young ears of fresh corn into pieces about 2 inches in length. Skewer corn and cook 10 minutes, brushing frequently with melted, seasoned butter.

4 servings

HAWAIIAN HAM KEBABS

Combine orange juice, butter, brown sugar, cloves, ginger, and orange rind; add ham and toss to coat. Cover and refrigerate at least 2 hours. Cut pineapple in chunks; peel and section oranges. Preheat grill element (grates removed), on "Hi" for 3 to 5 minutes: Drain ham; reserve marinade. Alternate ham, pineapple, and orange sections on skewers. Broil for 15 minutes, brushing frequently with marinade. Serve hot with rice or with baked sweet potatoes.

4 servings

1/4 cup orange juice
1/4 cup butter, melted
2 tablespoons brown sugar
10 cloves
2 teaspoons ginger
1 tablespoon grated orange rind
1 pound baked ham, cut in 2-inch cubes
1 fresh pineapple, or 16 chunks canned pineapple, drained
1 orange

ITALIAN SAUSAGE KEBABS

2 cups marinara sauce, or 1 jar (15 1/2 ounces) prepared marinara sauce
1/3 cup of dry white wine
2 teaspoons soy sauce
2 or 3 summer squash, unpeeled
1/2 teaspoon salt
12 firm cherry tomatoes
1 pound mild (sweet) sausage, cut into 1 1/4-inch pieces
1 cup very finely shredded mozzarella cheese (optional)

In a small bowl, combine marinara sauce, wine, and soy sauce. Rinse the squash and cut into 3/4-inch slices. Sprinkle with salt and set aside. Wash and dry tomatoes; remove stems. Preheat grill element (grates removed) on "Hi" for 3 to 5 minutes. Alternate slices of sausage and squash on 3 skewers (skewer squash through skins). Arrange cherry tomatoes on fourth skewer. Broil the skewers of sausage and squash on "10" for 30 minutes. Baste frequently with marinara sauce. Add skewer of tomatoes 15 minutes before sausage and squash are done. Heat the reserved marinara sauce and let it simmer for 5 minutes. Serve kebabs over rice; sprinkle kebabs with shredded mozzarella cheese while still hot. Pass marinara sauce. Italian bread and a green salad dressed with oil and vinegar complete a hearty meal.

4 servings

Nice to know: To make marinara sauce at home, combine 1 1/2 cups canned tomatoes, 1 chopped medium-size onion, 1 minced clove garlic, 1 tablespoon olive oil, 3 tablespoons of tomato paste, 1 teaspoon salt, 1/4 teaspoon oregano, 1/2 teaspoon basil, and a dash pepper with 1/4 cup water. Process at medium speed in a blender; simmer, covered, for 20 to 30 minutes. Boil fairly briskly for 5 minutes uncovered. This sauce is very good on pasta; double the recipe if you would like to freeze some for future use; it keeps well.

VEAL KEBABS

In large bowl, combine wine, butter, tomato juice, basil, oregano, salt, and pepper. Add veal and toss to coat; cover and refrigerate at least 1 hour. Combine oil, lemon juice, parsley, and garlic in a bowl. Add mushrooms and peppers; cover and let stand at room temperature 1 hour. Preheat grill element (grates removed), on "Hi" for 3 to 5 minutes. Drain veal and vegetables; reserve the marinades. Arrange veal cubes on 2 skewers, peppers and mushrooms separately on the other 2 skewers. Broil skewers of veal in center positions for 30 minutes; baste frequently with the wine-butter mixture. Ten minutes before veal is done, add the skewer of green peppers to one of the outside positions; 5 minutes before the veal is done, add the skewer of mushrooms to the other outside position. Baste the vegetables frequently with lemon juice-oil mixture while they broil. Serve hot over a bed of rice.

4 servings

1/2 cup dry white wine
5 tablespoons butter, melted
1/4 cup tomato juice
1/2 teaspoon basil
1/2 teaspoon oregano
1/2 teaspoon salt
Pepper
1 pound boneless veal shoulder, cut into 3/4-inch cubes
3 tablespoons vegetable oil
3 tablespoons lemon juice
1 teaspoon dry parsley
1 clove garlic, minced, or 2 teaspoons minced dry garlic
12 large mushroom caps
2 green peppers, cut into 1-inch squares

GREEK LAMB KEBABS

1/2 cup tarragon vinegar
1/2 cup olive oil, divided
1/2 teaspoon basil
  2 cloves garlic, crushed
     Freshly ground pepper
1 1/2 pounds boned leg of
       lamb, cut into
       1 1/2-inch cubes
1/2 cup tomato juice
  2 tablespoons lemon juice
  2 tablespoons soy sauce
1/2 teaspoon crushed
     red pepper
  1 large eggplant, unpeeled,
     cut into 1-inch cubes

Combine vinegar, 1/4 cup oil, basil, garlic, and pepper to taste. Add lamb and toss to coat. Cover and refrigerate at least 2 hours or overnight. Combine remaining 1/4 cup oil, tomato juice, lemon juice, soy sauce, and red pepper. Add eggplant and toss to coat; cover and refrigerate at least 2 hours. Preheat grill element (grates removed), on "Hi" for 3 to 5 minutes. Alternate lamb and eggplant on skewers. Broil for 30 minutes; serve hot with rice or wheat pilaf.

Note: Eggplant will be firm and crisp. If softer eggplant is preferred, parboil eggplant cubes in boiling salted water for 5 minutes before placing in marinade.

4 servings

LEMON-CHICKEN KEBABS

1/2 cup tomato sauce
1/4 cup dry vermouth or
     dry white wine
  2 tablespoons butter,
     melted
  4 tablespoons lemon
     juice, divided
1/2 teaspoon salt
     Pepper
  1 tablespoon tarragon
  1 bay leaf
  2 chicken breasts,
     boned, skinned, and
     cut into
     1 1/2-inch pieces
 12 small white onions
  1 teaspoon salt
  2 lemons, cut in wedges
  1 can (8 ounces)
     cranberry sauce
  2 tablespoons orange
     juice

In large bowl, combine tomato sauce, vermouth, butter, 2 tablespoons lemon juice, salt, pepper, tarragon, and bay leaf; add chicken pieces; toss to coat; cover and refrigerate at least 2 hours. Place peeled onions in boiling salted water; boil 5 minutes; drain. Preheat grill element (grates removed), on "10" for 3 to 5 minutes. Arrange chicken pieces on 2 skewers; alternate onions and lemon wedges on the other 2 skewers. Place chicken skewers in the center positions and broil for 30 minutes. During the last 10 minutes add skewers of onions and lemons in the outside positions. In small saucepan, combine cranberry sauce, remaining 2 tablespoons lemon juice, and orange juice; heat until melted and smooth.

To serve: Place chicken and onions in center of platter. Squeeze juice from 2 lemon wedges over chicken. Garnish with remaining lemon wedges. Serve sauce in a bowl.

4 servings

Greek Lamb Kebabs

SCALLOP KEBABS

1/2 cup seasoned bread
    crumbs
5 tablespoons melted
    butter, divided
2 tablespoons sesame
    seed, toasted
1 tablespoon paprika
1 pound fresh sea
    scallops
1 clove garlic, crushed
    Salt and pepper
12 cherry tomatoes
2 green peppers, cut
    into 1-inch squares

In small bowl, combine bread crumbs, 2 table-spoons melted butter, sesame seed, and paprika. Coat scallops with bread-crumb mixture. Preheat grill element (grates removed) on "Hi" for 3 to 5 minutes. Combine remaining 3 tablespoons melted butter, garlic, salt, and pepper. Arrange scallops on 2 skewers; alternate cherry tomatoes and green peppers on the other 2 skewers. Broil scallops 30 minutes in center positions. Baste frequently with seasoned butter. Fifteen minutes before scallops are done, add the vegetable skewers in the outside positions. Serve hot with lemon wedges. Steamed spinach would be very good with these kebabs.

4 servings

Nice to know: If firm, evenly shaped scallops are not available, eliminate sesame seeds from coating mixture and wrap coated scallops with 1/2 slice of partially cooked bacon. This will help hold scallops securely on skewer. Basting with seasoned butter during cooking will not be necessary.

SWEET AND SOUR SHRIMP KEBABS

1/2 cup pineapple juice
1/2 cup orange juice
1/4 cup lemon juice
1/3 cup firmly packed
    brown sugar
2 tablespoons soy sauce
2 tablespoons cider vinegar
2 tablespoons prepared
    mustard
1 teaspoon salt
1 pound large fresh shrimp,
    peeled and deveined
1 fresh pineapple, cut
    into 1-inch cubes,
    or 16 chunks canned
    pineapple, drained
2 green peppers, cut
    into 1-inch squares
1 tablespoon cornstarch

In bowl, combine pineapple juice, orange juice, lemon juice, brown sugar, soy sauce, vinegar, mustard, and salt; mix well. Add shrimp and toss to coat. Cover and refrigerate at least 2 hours. Preheat grill element (grates removed) on "Hi" for 3 to 5 minutes. Alternate shrimp, pineapple, and green pepper on skewers. Broil for 15 minutes, brushing with marinade frequently. Remove to serving platter. Pour marinade into small saucepan. Dissolve cornstarch in 1 tablespoon water; add to marinade. Simmer, stirring constant-ly, until slightly thickened. Serve over shrimp, pineapple, and green peppers.

4 servings

FRUIT KEBABS

Combine honey, lemon juice, ginger, and cinnamon in large bowl. Peel, seed, and quarter apples. Add to bowl. Peel, cut in half, and pit peaches. Add to bowl. Peel and cut bananas in quarters, wash grapes, and combine with other fruit. Toss to coat fruit. Preheat grill element (grates removed) on "Hi" for 3 to 5 minutes. Alternate apples, peaches, bananas, and grapes on skewers. Put skewer through center of apple chunks and peach halves, lengthwise through bananas and grapes. Broil for 10 to 12 minutes, or until heated through, basting frequently. Serve hot as an accompaniment to meat or as a warm dessert.

Note: For a very special dessert, place cooked skewered fruit on a large platter. Pour 1/4 cup warmed brandy over the skewers. Very carefully flame. When the flames go out, serve with ice cream.

4 to 6 servings

1/4 cup honey
3 tablespoons lemon juice
1/4 teaspoon ginger
1/4 teaspoon cinnamon
2 cooking apples, such as McIntosh or Rome Beauty
4 small peaches
2 large, very firm bananas
16 large seedless grapes

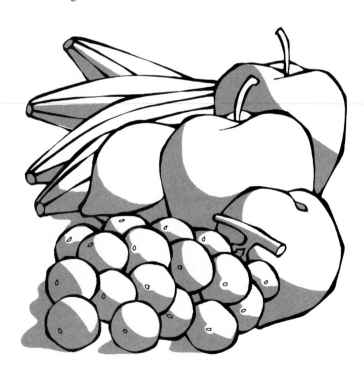

JENN-AIR FRENCH FRYER/COOKER

The Jenn-Air French fryer/cooker may soon become your favorite accessory. Its broad, shallow shape makes it possible to deep-fry food without crowding and to retrieve it easily and quickly when it is done. The French fryer is also a stew pot. Beans, stew, soup, chili, and sauces are easy to make in the fryer since it features a cover and the capacity to hold a really big batch of food.

The fryer should be filled to the oil mark (3 quarts of oil) for best deep-frying results. Use the thermometer to be sure the oil is at the proper temperature for the food to be fried. You may find considerable variation in the time it takes to heat the oil. Allow at least 25

to 35 minutes for the oil to reach 350°. Use good quality vegetable oil for frying. It can be cooled, strained, stored, and used several times. Frequent skimming to remove food particles that collect in the oil helps keep it fresh and clear. (Tie several layers of cheesecloth over a long-handled slotted spoon to make an instant skimmer.) Fry slices of raw potato (discard them later) in oil to eliminate food flavors after preparing your recipe. Always refrigerate oil between uses. When oil is reused, some new oil will have to be added each time to make up for the amount absorbed by the previous frying food. Discard oil when it foams, turns dark, or fails to brown food properly.

When you fry several batches of food, let the oil come back to the specified temperature between batches. It is a good idea to let food to be fried come to room temperature before it is added to the oil. That way the cooling effect of adding food will be lessened.

Raw food should always be dried thoroughly before frying and frozen foods, such as French fries or shrimp, should be free of ice crystals before they are immersed in hot oil. Moisture (or ice) will make the fat spatter. It's a good idea to wear an oven mitt when using the French fryer; some spatters are just about inevitable, and your hands should be protected.

Immerse the basket slowly in the oil. Lift it occasionally and shake it during frying to prevent the food from sticking; it is especially important to shake the basket when French-frying potatoes. Drain excess oil from food by hooking the basket on the sides of the fryer. Drain food further on paper towels. When frying batter-coated food, use tongs to lower batter-coated food gently into the oil. Don't use the basket since the batter tends to stick to it. Don't crowd the fryer with food, and give an extra margin of room to batter-covered foods so they won't stick to each other.

Foods	Oil Temperature	Approximate Frying Time
Doughnuts	370°	2 to 5 minutes
Fritters	370° to 375°	3 to 5 minutes
Croquettes (cooked food)	350°	2 to 3 minutes
(uncooked food)	370°	5 to 6 minutes
French Fried Potatoes	370°	6 to 8 minutes
French Fried Onions	370°	2 to 3 minutes
Chicken	365°	10 to 15 minutes
	375°	6 to 8 minutes
Fish Fillets	370°	2 to 3 minutes
Shrimp, raw or cooked	350° to 375°	2 to 3 minutes
Oysters, Clams	370°	2 to 3 minutes
Veal or Pork Cutlets	380°	6 to 8 minutes

CHINESE EGG ROLLS

Heat oil in French fryer on "Hi" to 350°. To make pancakes, beat eggs slightly in small bowl. Blend in flour, cornstarch, 2 cups water, and salt. Heat a 7- or 8-inch skillet until a drop of water "dances" on the surface. Grease skillet and pour in about 2 tablespoons batter. Tilt skillet so batter coats bottom of pan. Cook on one side only. Pancakes should not brown. Combine remaining ingredients in small bowl. Place about 1 tablespoon of seafood mixture on cooked side of pancake. Fold over opposite sides of pancake from left to right and then roll up from bottom to top. Moisten the edges with a little water to seal very securely. Fry a few egg rolls at a time for about 2 minutes, or until lightly browned. Drain on paper towels and serve.

Oil for deep-fat frying
3 eggs
1 cup all-purpose flour
2 tablespoons cornstarch
1/2 teaspoon salt
1 cup chopped cooked shrimp or crabmeat
1/2 cup chopped celery
1/3 cup cooked crumbled bacon
2 tablespoons chopped onion
1 can (16 ounces) mixed Chinese vegetables
1 tablespoon soy sauce

12 servings

Nice to know: If you want to try this recipe when your time is limited, you can buy egg roll skins in specialty food stores. Store them in your freezer, ready to use at any time.

SCOTCH EGGS

Heat oil in French fryer on "Hi" to 350°. Combine sausage, anchovies, 1/2 cup bread crumbs, and raw egg in large bowl. Press mixture together to form coat on hard-cooked eggs. Combine remaining 1/2 cup bread crumbs and parsley. Dip coated eggs in beaten egg and then in bread-crumb mixture. Fry a few eggs at a time for at least 5 minutes, or until well browned. (Remember, pork must be cooked thoroughly!) Drain on paper towels and serve.

Oil for deep-fat frying
1 pound pork sausage
3 anchovies, mashed
1 cup dry bread crumbs, divided
1 egg
6 hard-cooked eggs
2 tablespoons chopped parsley
1 egg, slightly beaten

6 servings

MASHED POTATO PUFFS

Oil for deep-fat frying
1 cup soft mashed
   potatoes
1 egg
1/2 cup all-purpose flour
1 teaspoon baking
   powder
1/4 teaspoon salt
2 tablespoons minced
   onion
1 tablespoon grated
   Parmesan cheese
1 teaspoon chopped
   parsley

Heat oil in French fryer on "Hi" to 350°. Combine all ingredients in small bowl; mix thoroughly. Drop by tablespoonsful into hot oil. Fry about 3 to 4 minutes, or until browned. Drain on paper towels and serve immediately.

Note: Smaller puffs (made by frying teaspoonsful of potato mixture) make interesting hors d'oeuvre. Serve with toothpicks and spicy tomato sauce for dipping.

4 servings

CHICKEN KIEV

Oil for deep-fat frying
1 stick (1/2 cup) butter
2 tablespoons chopped
   chives
2 tablespoons chopped
   parsley
4 chicken breasts, boned,
   skinned, and halved
1 egg
3/4 cup dry bread crumbs

Heat oil in French fryer on "Hi" to 350°. Cut butter in half lengthwise and then into 8 equal pieces. Combine chives and parsley. Roll each piece of butter in chive mixture. Cut chicken breasts in half and pound until thin. Place a piece of butter in center of each breast. Fold over and roll up so butter is completely enclosed. Secure with toothpicks. Beat egg with 2 tablespoons of water. Dip chicken rolls in egg mixture and then in bread crumbs. Fry a few chicken breasts at a time for about 3 to 4 minutes, or until browned. Drain on paper towels and serve immediately.

8 servings

BEER-BATTER FRIED CHICKEN

Oil for deep-fat frying
3/4 cup all-purpose flour
3/4 teaspoon salt
1/4 teaspoon pepper
3/4 cup beer
1 broiler-fryer
   chicken, cut into
   serving pieces

Heat oil in French fryer on "Hi" to 350°. Combine flour, salt, pepper, and beer in small bowl. Allow to stand at room temperature 30 minutes. Dip chicken pieces into batter, coating thoroughly. Fry a few pieces at a time for about 20 to 30 minutes, or until cooked. (Larger chicken pieces may take longer to cook.) Drain on paper towels and serve immediately.

4 servings

Chicken Kiev

TEMPURA

Oil for deep-fat frying
10 raw jumbo shrimp,
    shelled and deveined
1 egg
6 tablespoons
    all-purpose flour
2 tablespoons cornstarch
1/4 teaspoon baking powder
4 large mushrooms, cut
    in half
1 yam, peeled and cut
    into 1/8-inch slices
1/2 small head cauliflower,
    cut into flowerets
1 green pepper, cut
    into 1/4-inch rings
2 small zucchini, cut
    into 1/4-inch strips
1 medium-size sweet
    Spanish onion,
    sliced

Heat oil in French fryer on "Hi" to 350°. Cut shrimp down back, almost through. Flatten out. In small bowl, beat egg and 1/2 cup water. Add flour, cornstarch, and baking powder; stir until smooth. Dip shrimp and vegetable pieces into batter and fry until lightly browned on both sides. Drain on paper towels and serve with individual bowls of Sweet-Sour Sauce.

Note: Most vegetables are very good cooked by this method. You might like to try broccoli, green beans, cherry tomatoes, curly parsley sprigs, and 1-inch whole peeled onions that have been parboiled for 5 minutes and thoroughly dried.

2 servings

Sweet-Sour Sauce

1/2 cup pineapple juice
3 tablespoons vegetable
    oil
2 tablespoons brown
    sugar
1 teaspoon soy sauce
1/4 cup vinegar

Heat ingredients in small sauce pan. Serve with Tempura.

SALMON CROQUETTES

Drain salmon thoroughly, remove bones, and flake fish. Melt butter in saucepan over medium heat. Blend in 3 tablespoons of the flour. Gradually add 1 cup milk and continue stirring until thickened. Add salt, lemon juice, and Worcestershire. Pour a small amount of hot mixture into beaten egg yolks and return all to saucepan. Cook, stirring, about 1 minute. (Do not boil.) Stir in onion, salmon, soft bread crumbs and parsley. Transfer mixture to flat pan, cover, and chill 1 hour. Heat oil in French fryer on "Hi" to 350°. Divide salmon mixture into 12 parts. Form each part into a cone shape and roll in the remaining 4 tablespoons flour. Beat together remaining milk and egg. Roll each cone in egg mixture and then in bread crumbs. Fry croquettes about 2 minutes, or until browned. Drain on paper towels and serve immediately with a flavored mayonnaise or a béchamel sauce.

6 servings

1 can (16 ounces) salmon
3 tablespoons butter or margarine
7 tablespoons all-purpose flour, divided
1 1/8 cups milk, divided
3/4 teaspoon salt
2 teaspoons lemon juice
1 teaspoon Worcestershire sauce
2 egg yolks, beaten
2 tablespoons finely minced onion
1 3/4 cups soft bread crumbs
2 teaspoons chopped parsley
Oil for deep-fat frying
1 egg
3/4 cup dry bread crumbs

FISH AND CHIPS

Cut fish fillets into serving-size pieces. Sprinkle with salt and pepper to taste and set aside. Combine flour, eggs, milk, paprika, and cayenne; blend well. Heat oil in French fryer on "Hi" to 350°. Cut potatoes into slices about 1/8 inch thick. Fry potatoes until golden brown, about 5 minutes. Remove, drain, and keep warm. Dip fish pieces into batter. Fry about 1 1/2 minutes, or until golden. Drain on paper towels and serve immediately.

6 servings

2 pounds flounder fillets
Salt and pepper
1 cup all-purpose flour
2 eggs
1/3 cup milk
1/2 teaspoon paprika
1/8 teaspoon cayenne
Oil for deep-fat frying
6 medium-size potatoes, peeled

BASIC FRITTERS

Oil for deep-fat frying
1 1/4 cups all-purpose flour
1 teaspoon baking
    powder
1/2 teaspoon salt
1 cup milk
1 tablespoon melted
    butter
2 eggs

Heat oil in French fryer on "Hi" to 370°. Sift dry ingredients into bowl. Add milk, butter, and eggs; mix well. Drop batter by teaspoonfuls into hot fat. Use a rubber spatula to push batter off teaspoon with minimum spatter. Fry fritters until golden brown on both sides, about 2 to 4 minutes. Drain on paper towels and serve hot.

VARIATIONS:

Corn Fritters

Decrease milk in basic recipe to 1/2 cup. Then add 1 1/2 cups cooked cut corn or 1 can (12 ounces) whole-kernel corn, drained. Stir corn into batter and fry according to basic recipe instructions.

Apple Cinnamon Fritters

Stir 1/4 cup sugar, 1 1/2 cups chopped apples, and 1/4 teaspoon cinnamon into basic fritter batter. Deep fry according to basic recipe instructions.

Banana Fritters

Add 2 tablespoons sugar, 1/2 teaspoon vanilla extract, and 1 teaspoon grated orange peel to basic fritter batter. Cut 3 firm peeled bananas in half lengthwise, then crosswise. Dip banana pieces in lemon juice and then into batter. Fry a few at a time for 1 to 1 1/2 minutes, or until very lightly browned.

Rum Puffs

Add 2 tablespoons rum, 2 tablespoons sugar, and a dash of salt to basic batter. Drop by tablespoons into hot oil and fry about 1 minute, or until golden brown.

6 to 8 servings

SWEET RICE FRITTERS

Heat oil in French fryer on "Hi" to 350°. Combine all ingredients; blend well. Drop mixture by tablespoonfuls into hot oil. Fry about 2 minutes, or until browned. Drain on paper towels and sprinkle with confectioners sugar.

6 servings

Nice to know: Lemon Sauce (page 157) is very good served with these unusual fritters.

> Oil for deep-fat frying
> 1 cup all-purpose flour
> 2 tablespoons sugar
> 1 teaspoon baking powder
> 1/2 teaspoon salt
> 3 eggs, slightly beaten
> 1/2 cup milk
> 2 tablespoons vegetable oil
> 2 cups cooked rice
> 1 teaspoon grated lemon peel
> 1/2 cup chopped walnuts
> Confectioners sugar

CROUTONS

When your French fryer is in use, you can easily make homemade croutons. The oil should be at 350° to fry them. You might make them as the oil heats to a higher temperature for another dish, or as the last project after your main cooking is done. Croutons are a good way to use up leftover bread; they keep indefinitely in the freezer and for up to 2 weeks in the refrigerator.

Heat oil in French fryer on "Hi" to 350°. Fry bread cubes about 1 minute, or until browned. Immediately toss with salt. Drain thoroughly on paper towels.

> Day-old white bread, cut into 1/2-inch cubes (3 slices make about 4 servings of croutons)
> 1/2 teaspoon salt

Seasoned Croutons

Combine all ingredients. Toss with fried croutons and salt as above. Drain thoroughly and store tightly covered.

> 2 tablespoons Parmesan cheese, grated
> 1 tablespoon finely chopped parsley
> 1/2 teaspoon paprika

RAISED DOUGHNUTS

5 to 6 cups all-purpose
flour, divided
1 cup sugar
2 packages active dry
yeast
1 teaspoon salt
1/3 cup butter or
margarine
1 1/4 cups milk
3 eggs, at room
temperature
Oil for deep-fat frying
Confectioners sugar

Combine 1 1/2 cups flour, sugar, yeast, and salt in large bowl of heavy duty electric mixer. Heat butter and milk to 120° to 130°. Add milk mixture to dry ingredients. Beat in eggs and beat 2 minutes at medium speed. Add 1 cup flour and beat 2 minutes at high speed. Stir in enough additional flour to make a soft dough. Turn out onto lightly floured surface and knead 8 to 10 minutes. Place in greased bowl and turn to grease top. Cover with clean towel and let rise in warm place (85°) until double in bulk, about 1 hour. Punch down. Place on floured surface and let rest, covered, 15 minutes. Divide dough in half. Roll dough out 1/4 inch thick. Cut rounds with a 3-inch doughnut cutter. Place on greased baking sheet. Cover and let rise 1 hour. Heat oil in French fryer on "Hi" to 370°. Fry 4 or 5 doughnuts at a time for about 1 minute. Turn once. Drain on paper towels and cool. Sprinkle with confectioners sugar.

VARIATIONS:

Old-Fashioned Doughnuts
Prepare dough as directed, adding 1/2 teaspoon nutmeg to batter. Roll out as directed with a doughnut cutter, or use the biscuit cutter and remove small circle for the hole. Fry as directed (including the "holes"). Roll in cinnamon-sugar when cool, if desired.

Honey Glazed Doughnuts
Combine 2/3 cup honey and 1/3 cup water in saucepan; heat until blended. Chill. Prepare dough as directed for Raised Doughnuts. Do not knead, but let rise. Stir dough down and drop by teaspoonful into hot oil. Drain. Dip doughnuts into chilled honey mixture. Let dry on wire racks.

Jelly Doughnuts
Cut dough with a 3-inch biscuit cutter. When doughnuts are finished frying, drain and cool. Make a small slit in side of each doughnut and fill with 2 teaspoons of jelly or preserves.

40 doughnuts

Old-Fashioned Doughnuts
Honey Glazed Doughnuts

QUICK DROP DOUGHNUTS

Oil for deep-fat frying
2 eggs
1/2 cup sugar
2 tablespoons
  shortening
2 cups all-purpose
  flour
2 teaspoons baking powder
1/4 teaspoon salt
1/4 teaspoon nutmeg

Heat oil in French fryer on "Hi" to 370°. Beat eggs until light and lemon colored; add sugar and shortening. Mix well. Sift together flour, baking powder, and salt. Add nutmeg and 1/2 cup water to egg mixture; add dry ingredients. Beat well. Spoon batter by teaspoonfuls into hot fat. A rubber spatula is convenient to push batter off spoon with minimum spatter. Turn to brown both sides. Remove from fat with slotted spoon and drain on paper towels. Shake, a few at a time, in a paper bag with 1/3 cup sugar combined with 2 teaspoons cinnamon. Store in a tightly covered container.

VARIATION:

Orange Doughnuts

Substitute 1/2 cup orange juice for water and add 1 tablespoon grated orange rind. Omit nutmeg.

36 1½-inch doughnuts

DEEP-FRIED CAMEMBERT OR GRUYERE

Oil for deep-fat frying
1 egg
2 tablespoons
  all-purpose flour
1/2 teaspoon salt
  Dash pepper
1 package (6 ounces)
  Camembert or Gruyère
  cheese, cut in wedges

Heat oil in French fryer on "Hi" to 350°. Combine egg, flour, salt, and pepper in small bowl. Dip cheese wedges in batter, coating throughly. Fry, being careful not to crowd fryer, about 1 1/2 minutes, or until golden brown. Drain on paper towels. Serve immediately for dessert with chilled grapes and crisp apple slices.

4 servings

PARTY FRICASSEE

Wash and dry the chicken pieces and dust with salt and pepper. Melt butter in French fryer on "10." Add the chicken pieces and sauté until lightly browned, about 5 or 6 minutes on each side. Do not crowd chicken; do it in several batches if necessary. Set browned chicken aside. Add carrots, onions, and celery to fryer. Sauté, stirring occasionally, until onion is soft. Stir in flour and cook, stirring constantly, to blend. Add chicken broth all at once. Stir until mixture thickens. Reduce heat to "6" and return chicken to fryer with parsley and bay leaf. Cook gently, covered, until chicken is very tender, about 20 to 30 minutes. While the chicken cooks, peel onions and parboil them 5 minutes in lightly salted water. Wipe mushroom caps. Sauté parboiled onions, well drained, and mushrooms in a little butter or oil with a pinch of sugar for 5 minutes, stirring constantly. Five minutes before the chicken is done, add the onions and mushrooms to the fryer. Increase heat to "10." Mix the egg yolks with the cream and stir until combined. Very slowly beat about 2 cups of the hot gravy into the egg-cream mixture. Then return all to the fryer and heat, stirring constantly, until gravy thickens. Do not allow the sauce to boil or it will curdle. Season with lemon juice and nutmeg and taste for salt and pepper. Serve over hot homemade noodles for a special treat. Rice is nice, too.

8 to 10 servings

3 frying chickens (3 pounds each), cut into serving pieces
1 teaspoon salt
1/2 teaspoon white pepper
1 stick (1/4 pound) butter
3 carrots, thinly sliced
2 medium-size onions, thinly sliced
3 stalks celery, thinly sliced
5 tablespoons all-purpose flour
6 cups boiling chicken broth
1/4 cup chopped parsley or 1 teaspoon dry parsley
1 bay leaf
20 1-inch onions
20 1-inch mushroom caps
4 egg yolks
1 cup heavy cream
1 tablespoon lemon juice
Pinch nutmeg

LOUISIANA SEAFOOD GUMBO

4 tablespoons butter or
   margarine
1 cup chopped onions
1 clove garlic, minced,
   or 2 teaspoons
   minced dry garlic
2 quarts boiling water
1/2 cup long-grained rice
1 cup sliced celery
1 package (10 ounces)
   frozen okra, thawed
   and sliced
1 pound fresh shrimp,
   shelled and deveined,
   or 1 package
   (12 ounces) frozen
   deveined shrimp,
   thawed
1 can (28 ounces) tomatoes
1 green or red pepper,
   seeded and diced
3 tablespoons
   all-purpose flour
1/2 teaspoon thyme
1 1/2 teaspoons salt
1/2 teaspoon pepper
1/2 teaspoon hot pepper
   sauce
1 teaspoon
   Worcestershire sauce
1 bottle (8 ounces)
   clam juice
1 can (6 1/2 ounces)
   crab meat, boned,
   or 1 cup fresh
   cooked crab meat
1 can (2 ounces)
   pimiento, drained
   and diced

Melt butter in French fryer on "8"; sauté onion and garlic until lightly browned. Reduce heat to "4" and add water and rice. Cover and simmer gently for 20 minutes. Add celery, okra, shrimp, tomatoes, and green pepper; break up tomatoes with spoon. Cook on "6" another 20 minutes, or until vegetables and shrimp are tender. Blend flour, thyme, salt, pepper, hot pepper sauce, and Worcestershire with clam juice; stir to dissolve flour. Add to gumbo; stir until smooth. Add crab meat and pimiento and just heat through. Serve hot.

18 to 20 servings

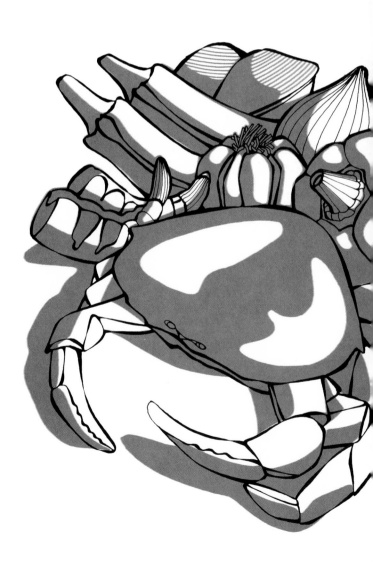

BEEF STEW

Melt butter in French fryer on "8." Mix flour, salt, pepper, and oregano in a paper bag. Add beef chunks and shake to coat. Brown meat on all sides in butter. Dredge onions in flour mixture and add to fryer to brown lightly. Add water or stock to fryer and stir to scrape all brown bits from bottom. Reduce temperature to "4" and simmer 30 minutes. Add carrots and potatoes. Tie garlic, bay leaf, celery, whole clove, and parsley sprigs in cheesecloth and add to pot. Simmer, covered, for 1 hour more. Remove spice bag and discard. Taste for seasonings; add soy sauce to taste. Serve in soup bowls sprinkled with chopped parsley.

6 to 8 servings

4 tablespoons butter
    or margarine
1/2 cup all-purpose flour
1 teaspoon salt
1 teaspoon pepper
1/2 teaspoon oregano
    (optional)
2 pounds stewing
    beef, cut in
    1 1/2-inch cubes
2 medium-size onions,
    roughly chopped
8 cups boiling water
    or stock
6 carrots, scraped and
    cut in 1-inch chunks
6 medium-size baking
    potatoes, washed,
    unpeeled, cut in
    quarters
2 cloves garlic, peeled
    and halved
1 bay leaf
1 cup chopped celery ribs
    and leaves
1 whole clove
4 or 5 sprigs parsley
    Soy sauce
    Chopped parsley for
    garnish

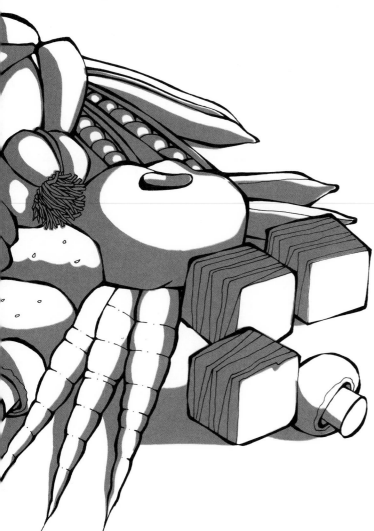

CHICKEN SOUP LOUIE

Wash and dry chicken and rub well with lemon inside and out. Place in French fryer. Add water to half cover chicken (about to deep-fat line). Cover and heat on "Hi" until boiling. Peel onions, leave whole, and push 2 cloves into each; add to chicken. Add remaining ingredients except garnish. Reduce heat to "4" and simmer for 1 1/2 to 2 hours, or until chicken is fork tender. When ready to serve, remove chicken and carve. Place meat in soup tureen, cover with broth, and garnish with parsley. Serve very hot.

6 to 8 servings

1 stewing chicken
   (3 to 4 pounds)
1/2 lemon
2 medium-size onions
4 cloves
1/2 cup thinly sliced celery
3 leeks, thinly sliced
1/2 cup diced carrots
1 tablespoon minced
   fresh parsley
1 bay leaf
2 teaspoons salt
1/4 teaspoon pepper
2 cups dry white wine
   Minced parsley

HOOSIER CORN CHOWDER

Fry bacon in French fryer on "8" until crisp and brown; remove bacon to paper towels. Crumble when cool and set aside. Reduce heat to "5"; add onion to drippings and sauté until transparent but not brown; add potatoes and water (water should cover potatoes). Cover fryer and simmer 20 to 25 minutes, or until tender. Add corn, milk, garlic powder, pepper, salt, pimiento, and hot pepper sauce. Cover and simmer another 20 minutes. Serve hot and pass crumbled bacon, minced parsley, and toasted croutons for toppings.

8 to 10 servings

6 slices bacon
1 cup chopped onions
4 cups diced potatoes
4 cups boiling water
3 cans (16 ounces each)
   cream-style corn or
   6 cups cooked cut corn
1 quart milk
1/4 teaspoon garlic powder
1/4 teaspoon white pepper
2 teaspoons salt
1 jar (2 ounces)
   pimiento, well
   drained and diced
   Dash hot pepper sauce
   Minced parsley
   Toasted croutons

Hoosier Corn Chowder

JENN-AIR SELECTIVE-USE CONVECTION OVEN

The convection oven is just about the greatest improvement in baking since electricity. Convection ovens have been used for years by bakeries and in restaurants, but only recently has Jenn-Air made the advantages of convection cooking available to home cooks. Convection ovens bake with constantly recirculating heated air driven by a concealed fan. The moving air strips away the natural thermal barriers that surround food. Foods cook faster and a few foods also cook at lower temperatures. Meat in particular will have a beautiful golden brown color while remaining juicy and tender inside. And convection baking makes it possible to make French bread at home.

Variety and Cut of Meat	Approximate Weight (Pounds)	Convection Oven Temperature (Not preheated) °F	Internal Temperature of Meat - End of Roasting Time °F	Approximate Roasting Time (minutes per pound)*
BEEF				
Rib Roast	4 to 6	325°	140° (rare)	24-26
			160° (medium)	29-31
Rib Roast	6 to 8	325°	140° (rare)	23-25
			160° (medium)	28-30
Rib Eye Roast	4 to 6	325°	140° (rare)	19-22
			160° (medium)	25-28
Top Sirloin Roast Special Cut	3 to 6	325°	140° (rare)	21-27
			160° (medium)	27-30
Loin Tenderloin Roast	3 to 4	325°	140° (rare)	20-25
Round Rump Roast, Boneless	4 to 6	325°	140° (rare)	23-28
			160° (medium)	30-35
Round Eye Round Roast	4 to 5	325°	140° (rare)	20-22
			160° (medium)	25-27
Round Tip Roast	4 to 6	325°	140° (rare)	20-25
			160° (medium)	26-31
Round Top Round Roast	3½ to 6	325°	140° (rare)	27-30
			160° (medium)	33-36
PORK				
Loin Sirloin Roast, Boneless	4 to 6	300°	170°	37-40
Loin Sirloin Roast, Bone-In	4 to 6	300°	170°	24-28
Shoulder Blade Roast, Boneless	3 to 5	325°	170°	36-39
Half ham, Boneless Fully cooked	5 to 7	325°	140°	18-23
Smoked Ham, Rump Portion, Cook-before eating	5 to 7	275°	160°	30-38
VEAL				
Shoulder Roast, Rolled Boneless	3 to 5	325°	170°	35-50
Rib Roast	5 to 7	325°	170°	23-30
Leg, Sirloin Roast, Boneless	4 to 7	325°	170°	25-40
Leg Rump Roast, Boneless	4 to 5	325°	170°	28-34
LAMB				
Shoulder Roast, Boneless	2½ to 6	325°	140° (rare)	25-27
			160° (medium)	30-32
			170° (well)	34-36
Leg, Whole	5 to 7	325°	140° (rare)	17-19
			160° (medium)	22-24
			170° (well)	25-27
Leg Roast, Boneless	4 to 6	325°	140° (rare)	20-25
			160° (medium)	25-30
			170° (well)	30-35
Leg Short Cut, Sirloin off	2 to 3	325°	140° (rare)	25-30
			160° (medium)	30-35
			170° (well)	35-40

*These times are for (unfrozen) meat taken directly from the refrigerator.

Variety and Cut of Meat	Approximate Weight (Pounds)	Convection Oven Temperature (Not preheated) °F	Internal Temperature of Meat - End of Roasting Time °F	Approximate Roasting Time (minutes per pound)*
POULTRY				
Fryer	2½ to 3½	375°	185°	17-20
Roasting chicken	4 to 6	325°	185°	20-26
Turkey, unstuffed	10 to 14	325°	185°	12-14
Turkey, unstuffed	14 to 18	325°	185°	10-12
Turkey, unstuffed	18 to 24	325°	185°	7-10

Cooking times and temperatures, as well as rack positions and sometimes the position of the food being cooked, are often quite different in convection ovens and radiant (conventional) ovens. The recipes in this book were developed and tested especially for the convection oven. Therefore, these directions will not work in a radiant oven. The differences in the two methods could lead to seriously underdone food and disappointment. Use standard cookbooks for the conventional radiant oven; *this book is for convection "mode" cooking only.*

Since the convection oven reaches its set temperature very quickly, preheating is rarely necessary. Recipes provide instructions about when to turn the oven on; follow these instructions carefully for best results and greatest economy.

Meat or poultry to be roasted in the convection oven should be placed on the rack in the roasting pan that comes with the oven or in a similar **shallow** pan. Do not add water to the roasting pan. A pan with high sides should *not* be used as it will prevent meat from browning evenly and slow the cooking process. Cuts of meat that contain a bone, such as ribs of beef or loin of pork, should be rested on the side; the fat layer should be turned toward the fan. Meat cooked in the convection oven will not need basting.

Do not cover poultry with aluminum foil; birds brown evenly and retain their juices when roasted in the convection oven.

Make a habit of consulting the roasting charts in this book for recommended cooking temperatures and times. Large cuts of meat will require fewer minutes per pound to roast than a smaller cut. And meat that is chunkier will roast slower than a flatter cut that weighs the same. Many meats, especially beef, continue to cook after being removed from the oven. It is a good idea to take the roast out when it reaches an internal temperature 5 to 10 degrees below the temperature desired. Allow the meat to stand 15 minutes before carving. (The minutes per pound given in the charts are for internal temperature reached while meat is in the oven.) Also note that minutes per pound may vary according to the electrical voltage in your area. For best results, use a meat thermometer for roasting and watch timing carefully to prevent overcooking.

Meat may be roasted frozen-to-finish in your convection oven. Use the temperatures recommended for unfrozen meat. Most roasting is done at 325°, and for best results do not use temperatures below 300°. In general, roasting times for frozen-to-finish in the convection oven will be approximately the same as fresh-to-finish in a radiant (conventional) oven. Use a meat thermometer to be sure of perfect results (insert it midway through the cooking process).

There are four rack positions in your Jenn-Air convection oven. The bottom one, or rack position 1, should be used for large cuts of meat, large cakes (such as angel food cake), and food that will rise considerably while baking. Rack position 2 is used for most other baking. Rack position 3 is good for some appetizers, breads, and most convenience foods. Rack position 4 is used for heating thin foods, such as pizzas, very quickly. Baking sheets should be placed in the center of the racks. Such placement insures even baking and browning and proper circulation of the heated air. For certain recipes, when multiple racks are used, it is a good idea to rotate the pans halfway through the cooking period. For example, for more even browning of cakes, pies, and certain hors d'oeuvres, reverse pans, front to back, top to bottom.

The racks not in use can be used as oversize extra cooling racks, especially helpful for large baking projects.

Product	Type	Pan Size	Convection Temp. °F Preheated	Rack Position	Convection Time
Cake	White - 2 layer	8 in.	325°	2	30-32
	Yellow - 2 layer	8 in.	350°	2	29-34
	Chocolate - 2 layer	8 in.	325°	2	41-45
	Bundt	tube	350°	2	45-50
	Angel Food	tube	325°	1	38-42
	Pineapple upside down	8 x 8	325°	2	32-35
	Pound Cake (loaf)	9 x 5	325°	2	52-55
	Snackin Cake	8 x 8	350°	2	24-26
	Coffee Cake - your recipe	9 in.	375°	2	25-27
Pies	Fruit - 2 crust	9 in.	400°	2	40-42
	Fruit lattice crust	9 in.	375°	2	35-37
	Pecan	9 in.	375°	2	36-38
Cookies	Chocolate Chip		375°	2	7
	Peanut Butter		375°	2	8
	Sugar		375°	2	8
	Brownies	9 x 9	350°	2	23
Breads & Rolls	Quick Bread Loaf	9 x 5	375°	2	37-40
	Frozen Bread dough	9 x 5	350°	2	24-27
	Brown & Serve Rolls		350°	2	10
	Corn Muffins		425°	2	12
	Bran Muffins		400°	2	19
	Biscuits - your recipe		450°	2	7
	Yeast Loaf	9 x 5	375°	2	21-25

Frozen Convenience Foods	Rack Position	Convection Oven		Recommended Radiant Oven	
		Minutes	Temp. °F	Minutes	Temp. °F
Fruit Pie	1	36-39	425°	45-55	425°
Macaroni & Cheese	2	38-40	425°	60	425°
Fried Chicken (Heat 'n Serve)	2	18	400°	25	400°
Asparagus Soufflé	3	55	350°	65-70	350°
Pot Pie	3	30-33	425°	35-40	425°
Chicken Divan	3	25-28	400°	35	400°
Lasagna with Meat Sauce	2	35-38	425°	50	425°
Fish Portions - Batter Fried	3	17	425°	25-30	425°
TV Dinners - Four	3	20	425°	35-40	425°

Convection baking retains moisture within the food, which is a benefit when cooking meat or food that might dry out in conventional baking. This characteristic may be a problem with cakes, cookies, and breads that are extra-rich or that have fruit added. They will probably take longer to bake in the convection mode. Therefore, radiant (conventional) baking is usually preferred for baked goods made from your own recipe, such as rich chocolate cake or bar cookies and fruit bread. If there is a question about which mode of baking to use, select the radiant mode.

Full meals can be prepared in the convection oven by timing each dish so everything will be ready at the same time. Some suggestions for oven meals are included with the recipes and you can adapt this method of cooking to your family's favorite combinations.

Before you begin to use your convection oven, be sure to study the owner's manual carefully. The Jenn-Air use and care guide provides much helpful information, cooking tips, and safety guides. Find a spot for it near your oven and refer to it often as you enter the wonderful world of Jenn-Air convection cooking.

APPETIZERS

MINI-QUICHES

Cook bacon until crisp; drain and crumble; set aside. Divide pastry in quarters. Roll each quarter into a 12-inch circle; cut 2 1/2- to 3 1/2- inch circles with a cookie cutter to fit tartlet pans. Fit dough into tartlet pans. (Use a small ball of dough to pat rolled dough into pans; the baked quiches will be easier to remove from pans.) Place tartlet pans on 2 cookie sheets. Sprinkle bacon, cheese, and scallion onto dough. Beat eggs, cream, salt, nutmeg, and pepper together and pour over the ingredients in the shell. Sprinkle with paprika. Bake in convection oven on rack positions 2 and 3 at 350° for 20 to 25 minutes, or until center of quiches is set. Rotate pans after 15 minutes.

40 servings

12	slices bacon
	Pastry for 2 double-crust 9-inch pies, unbaked
3/4	cup shredded Swiss cheese
1/4	cup finely chopped scallion
4	eggs
1 1/2	cups light cream
1/2	teaspoon salt
1/4	teaspoon nutmeg
1/4	teaspoon white pepper
	Paprika

TOMATOES STUFFED WITH CRAB MEAT

Remove stems and seeds from the cherry tomatoes. Drain for several minutes upside down on paper towels. Meanwhile, combine all remaining ingredients. Preheat convection oven to 375°. Fill drained tomatoes and place 2 or 3 tomatoes in each cup of a muffin tin or in custard cups set on a cookie sheet. Bake on rack position 2 for 5 minutes, or until browned. Serve hot.

30 servings

30	cherry tomatoes
1/4	cup mayonnaise
1	teaspoon minced onion
1/8	teaspoon thyme
1/4	teaspoon celery salt
1	can (6 1/2 ounces) crab meat, well drained
1/4	cup grated Parmesan cheese

Mini-Quiches
Tomatoes Stuffed with Crab Meat

SPICY BEEF MINIATURES

6 phyllo leaves
1 pound lean ground
    beef
2 tablespoons butter
    or margarine
1 small onion,
    finely chopped
2 cloves garlic, minced
1/2 teaspoon cinnamon
1/2 teaspoon coriander
1/2 teaspoon allspice
1 teaspoon salt
    Freshly ground pepper
1 can (8 ounces)
    tomato sauce
1/2 cup grated Parmesan
    cheese
1/4 cup butter, melted

Unroll phyllo leaves and place, flat, between slightly damp dish towels. Set aside. Brown the meat in a skillet. Drain and set aside. With a paper towel, wipe skillet and in it melt the 2 tablespoons of butter. Add onion and garlic and sauté until onion is softened but not browned. Add reserved beef, cinnamon, coriander, allspice, salt, and pepper; stir to combine. Stir in the tomato sauce and cheese and let simmer 20 minutes, stirring constantly or until thickened. Remove from heat and cool slightly. Place 1 sheet of phyllo dough on a large cutting board (keep remaining phyllo leaves covered with a damp towel). Cut the phyllo sheet into 6 strips and brush with melted butter. Place 1 teaspoon of beef filling on the bottom left hand corner of each strip. Fold each strip like a flag — pick up the bottom left corner (with the filling) and fold it to the right edge, making a triangle. Continue folding, keeping the shape of a triangle with each fold. Repeat process, using remaining filling and remaining leaves. Preheat convection oven to 350°. Place beef-filled triangles on ungreased baking sheet. Bake on rack position 2 (with the baking sheet centered on oven rack) 10-15 minutes, or until slightly golden. Cool on wire rack and serve.

36 servings

STUFFED MUSHROOMS

12 large mushrooms (about
    2 inches across)
3 tablespoons chopped onion
3 tablespoons butter
    or margarine
3 tablespoons fresh
    white bread crumbs
1/4 cup grated Swiss cheese
1/4 cup grated Parmesan
    cheese
4 tablespoons minced parsley
    or 1 tablespoon
    dry parsley
3 tablespoons light cream
    or milk

Remove stems from mushrooms; mince 3 tablespoons of stems (use remaining stems in other recipes). Sauté onion in butter until transparent. Add all ingredients except mushroom caps and mix thoroughly. Generously fill mushroom caps and place on cookie sheet. Bake in convection oven on rack position 2 at 375° for 20 minutes, or until cheese is melted and filling lightly browned. Serve hot.

Note: Stuffed mushrooms are an elegant side dish. To prepare while the meat bakes, lightly cover stuffed mushrooms with foil and bake on rack position 3 for the last 30 minutes the meat cooks.

12 servings

MINIATURE CREAM PUFFS

Follow recipe for Chocolate Eclairs (page 160) to make cream puff batter. Drop teaspoons of the batter onto a greased baking sheet, and bake, following eclair directions. As soon as puffs are done, slit tops and return to oven (now turned off) for 5 minutes to dry out a little inside. Cool completely before filling. Unfilled cream puffs may be stored for several days at room temperature in an airtight canister.

about 48 servings

FILLINGS
Ham Filling

Combine all ingredients and fill puffs. Filling looks decorative piped from a pastry bag.

3	cups finely chopped ham
1/3	cup minced sweet pickles
1/2	cup mayonnaise
1/2	teaspoon minced onion

Cheese Cucumber Filling

Peel, seed, and finely chop cucumbers; there should be 1 1/2 cups. Drain *very* thoroughly. Combine all ingredients and fill puffs.

2	medium-size cucumbers
1/2	cup finely chopped celery
1	package (3 ounces) cream cheese, softened
1/2	teaspoon minced onion
1/4	teaspoon salt
1/8	teaspoon pepper
1	teaspoon minced parsley

Other fillings that are good in miniature cream puffs include: chicken salad; shrimp salad; crab salad; leftover creamed foods (cut into tiny pieces); pâté; a combination of dairy sour cream, caviar (black or red), and chopped onion; sautéed minced fresh mushrooms flavored with onions and sherry; chopped hard-cooked eggs flavored with anchovy paste — the possibilities are endless.

HOT CRAB SPREAD

Combine all ingredients and put into a greased 2-cup baking dish or gratin dish. Bake in convection oven on rack position 2 at 350° for 20 minutes. Serve warm with crackers or melba toast.

1 1/2 cups

1	can (6 1/2 ounces) crab meat, well drained
1/2	cup mayonnaise
1	package (8 ounces) cream cheese
1/2	teaspoon Worcestershire sauce
2	drops hot pepper sauce

CRAB MEAT PUFFS

2 egg whites
1/2 cup mayonnaise
1 can (6 1/2 ounces) flaked crab meat
1/4 teaspoon paprika
1/4 teaspoon tarragon
1/2 teaspoon salt
30 cheese or rye crackers

Beat egg whites until stiff. Fold in remaining ingredients except crackers. Preheat convection oven to 375°. Spread crab mixture on crackers and place on baking sheet. Bake on rack position 3 for 5 minutes, or until puffy and brown. Serve hot.

30 servings

OLIVE APPETIZERS

1 cup grated sharp Cheddar cheese
2 tablespoons butter or margarine
1/2 cup all-purpose flour Freshly ground pepper
25 medium-size green pimiento-stuffed olives, drained

Cream together the cheese and butter; blend in flour and pepper. Knead dough until smooth. Put about 2 teaspoons of dough in the palm of one hand. Make a depression in the dough with your thumb, then place an olive in the depression. Form dough around olive so that it is completely covered. Bake finished olives on a cookie sheet in convection oven on rack position 3 for 15 minutes at 400°.

Note: These appetizers may be assembled several hours ahead and stored in the refrigerator, tightly covered, then baked as needed.

25 servings

JAMBALAYA CANAPES

2 scallions
1 clove garlic
1 thin slice gingerroot
1/2 cup chopped water chestnuts
1 egg white
1 1/2 teaspoons cornstarch
1 tablespoon dry sherry
1/4 teaspoon salt
1/2 pound medium-size cooked shrimp
9 slices white bread
1/4 cup butter or margarine, softened

Coarsely chop scallions, garlic, and gingerroot. Mix well with water chestnuts, egg white, cornstarch, sherry, and salt. Coarsely chop shrimp; add to mixture. Preheat convection oven to 375°. Remove crusts from bread; butter. Spread shrimp mixture on top and cut bread in half diagonally. Place on baking sheet on rack position 1 or 2 for 5 minutes, or until lightly browned. Serve hot.

18 servings

DEVILED HAM PUFFS

Mix together cream cheese, onion juice, baking powder, egg yolk, and salt. Cut rounds from the bread slices; toast on one side. Spread the untoasted side of the bread rounds first with deviled ham, then with the cheese mixture. Bake in convection oven on rack position 1 at 400° for 15 minutes. Serve hot.

* Make onion juice by grating onion with a very fine grater, or use bottled onion juice.

25 servings

1 package (8 ounces) cream cheese
1 tablespoon onion juice*
1/2 teaspoon baking powder
1 egg yolk
   Pinch salt
25 slices white bread
1 can (4 1/2 ounces) deviled ham

CHEESE SAUSAGE BALLS

Let all ingredients come to room temperature. Mix well and form into 1-inch balls. Bake on cookie sheet in convection oven on rack position 2 at 400° for 15 minutes. Serve hot.

Note: This recipe freezes well. Form balls, place on a cookie sheet, and freeze until firm. Then store frozen balls in an airtight bag to bake as needed.

about 50 servings

1 pound pork sausage
1 stick (10 ounces) sharp Cheddar cheese, grated
3 cups dry biscuit mix

SHERRIED CHEESE BITS

Combine all ingredients except crackers and mix well. Preheat convection oven to 375°. Spread cheese mixture on crackers and place on ungreased baking sheet. Bake on rack position 2 for 5 minutes, or until cheese is melted and brown. Serve hot.

20 servings

1 1/2 cups grated sharp Cheddar cheese
1/2 teaspoon prepared mustard
1/4 teaspoon garlic salt
1/4 teaspoon chili powder
1/4 cup dry sherry
20 melba toast crackers

LOUISIANA SHRIMP SPREAD

1/2 cup chopped onion
1/2 cup chopped green
    pepper
1 1/2 tablespoons butter
    or margarine
1 3/4 cups whole peeled
    tomatoes, canned or
    fresh, drained
1/2 cup crushed saltines
1/2 teaspoon salt
1/8 teaspoon pepper
1/4 teaspoon nutmeg
1/4 teaspoon thyme
1/4 teaspoon mace
  2 cans (4 1/2 ounces
    each) tiny shrimp
    or 1/2 pound fresh
    shrimp, cooked,
    shelled, and
    coarsely chopped

Sauté onion and green pepper in butter in skillet over medium heat until tender. Combine with remaining ingredients; mix well to break up tomatoes. Preheat convection oven to 375°. Pour shrimp mixture into shallow 1-quart casserole and bake on rack position 1 for 10 minutes, or until thoroughly heated. Serve hot with assorted crackers.

3 cups

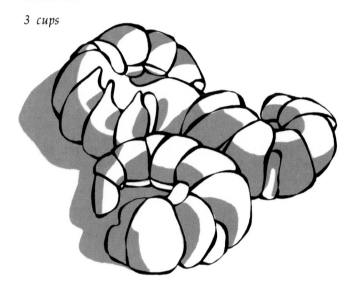

To prepare for a large party, there are several groups of hors d'oeuvre that can be made in the oven at the same time. You may like to try the following. Rotate appetizers on racks 1 and 3 after 10 minutes.

Cheese Sausage Balls (page 81)
Olive Appetizers (page 80)
Deviled Ham Puffs (page 81)

Another combination that will bake together is

Sherried Cheese Bits (page 81)
Crab Meat Puffs (page 80)
Jambalaya Canapes (page 80)
Louisiana Shrimp Spread (above)

You might heat the crackers or toast for the spread in the oven at the same time.

MEAT

SAUERBRATEN

Put roast in a large, deep bowl. Combine the next 10 ingredients with 2 cups water in a saucepan and bring to a boil. Simmer 5 minutes over low heat. Pour over roast and let cool. Cover tightly with plastic wrap; refrigerate 3 days. Turn meat daily.

Remove roast from marinade and place in a shallow 11×14-inch roasting pan. Strain marinade and discard vegetables. Pour marinade over meat. Bake in convection oven on rack position 2 at 350° for 2 hours, or until internal temperature of meat reaches 170°. Transfer meat to a platter and cover while making sauce.

Pour off drippings from roasting pan and skim fat. (There should be 1 1/2 cups defatted drippings; add beef broth if necessary to make up 1 1/2 cups.) Combine drippings with the flour dissolved in 1/2 cup water. Add gingersnap crumbs and cook over medium heat, stirring constantly, until thick. Strain sauce and return to pan to keep warm over low heat.

Carve the roast into 1/4-inch slices and arrange overlapping on a large platter. Spoon hot sauce over slices. Buttered noodles are the traditional accompaniment for Sauerbraten.

If you would like to serve the Sauerbraten at a later time, place the slices on an oven-proof platter or pan. Spoon sauce over slices. Cover and refrigerate 1 to 2 days. Heat, uncovered, on rack position 2 at 400° for 30 minutes when ready to serve.

6 to 8 servings

1 boneless beef rump roast (about 4 pounds)
2 cups dry red wine
1 cup red wine vinegar
2 tablespoons sugar
1/2 cup chopped carrots
1/2 cup chopped onion
1/2 cup chopped celery
1/2 teaspoon pepper
2 whole bay leaves
1 teaspoon salt
1/2 teaspoon allspice
2 tablespoons all-purpose flour
1/2 cup gingersnap crumbs

FRENCH COUNTRY-STYLE STUFFED CABBAGE

1 small head
   (about 2 pounds)
   savoy or
   green cabbage
6 slices bacon, diced
2 cups chopped onion
2 large cloves garlic,
   minced
1 cup chopped
   green pepper
1/2 teaspoon thyme
1 1/2 teaspoons salt
1/2 teaspoon pepper
1 can (16 ounces)
   stewed tomatoes,
   drained (reserve
   liquid)
2 pounds lean
   ground beef
2 eggs
4 slices white bread,
   torn into pieces
   Dairy sour cream

Place cabbage in a large pot and measure enough water to cover cabbage. Remove cabbage, add 1 tablespoon salt to water, cover, and bring to a boil. Return cabbage to pot and bring to a boil. Cook, uncovered, 10 minutes. Drain cabbage and cool under cold running water until cool enough to handle. Set aside. Place bacon in a large skillet and when it starts to sizzle, add onion, garlic, and green pepper. Sauté 5 minutes until onion is transparent. Remove skillet from heat and stir in thyme, salt, pepper, tomatoes, beef, eggs, and bread. Butter a 2-quart stainless steel bowl or round oven-proof casserole. Turn cabbage, core up, and remove core with a sharp knife. Gently pull cabbage leaves away from head and set aside. Line bottom of bowl with 2 or 3 large outer leaves, covering at least half the surface of the bowl. Spread some stuffing over leaves and continue adding leaves and stuffing until both are used up. The final layer should be cabbage leaves. Pour stewed tomato liquid over cabbage and cover tightly. Place bowl in convection oven on rack position 2 and bake at 450° for 30 minutes. Reduce oven temperature to 350° and bake 1 to 1 1/4 hours longer, or until meat thermometer inserted in center of cabbage registers 165°. Cool 10 minutes before unmolding. To unmold, drain liquid from bowl into saucepan and reserve. Run a small sharp knife between cabbage and inside of bowl to loosen. Invert serving platter over bowl and re-invert cabbage onto plate. Skim fat from pan liquid and heat. Cut cabbage in wedges to serve. Spoon some of the pan liquid over each serving and pass a bowl of sour cream separately.

Another way: Add 1 can (8 ounces) stewed tomatoes to skimmed liquid in saucepan before reheating.

8 to 10 servings

CRANBERRY BEEF ROAST

2 tablespoons
     vegetable oil
1 boneless chuck roast
     (3 to 4 pounds)
3/4 teaspoon salt
1/4 teaspoon cracked
     pepper
1 medium-size onion,
     sliced
1 teaspoon
     Worcestershire sauce
1/4 cup lemon juice
1 can (16 ounces)
     whole-berry
     cranberry sauce

Heat oil in skillet and brown meat on both sides. Remove meat to oven-proof pan with cover. Sprinkle with salt and pepper. In skillet sauté onion until lightly browned; add Worcestershire, lemon juice, and 1/2 cup water. Add to meat. Spread half the cranberry sauce on meat. Cover and bake in convection oven on rack position 2 at 300° for 1 hour and 30 minutes. Spread remaining cranberry sauce on meat and bake 1 hour more, or until fork tender. Add more water if necessary. Uncover for the last 15 minutes. Serve hot with cranberries on top. Skim fat from drippings and serve hot in a sauce boat.

6 to 8 servings

SAVORY POT ROAST

1 beef brisket
     (about 4 pounds)
2 1/2 cups Madeira, divided
     Salt and freshly
     ground pepper
2 bay leaves
1/2 teaspoon thyme
1/2 teaspoon basil
12 small white onions
8 carrots
1 1/4 cups all-purpose
     flour

Preheat convection oven to 400°. Place meat on baking sheet on rack position 4 and brown on both sides (about 4 minutes per side). Remove from oven and transfer to 5-quart dutch oven. Reset temperature to 325°. Combine 2 cups Madeira, 1/2 cup water, salt, pepper, bay leaves, thyme, and basil. Pour over beef. Cover and bake 1 hour. Add onions and carrots. Cover and bake 1 hour longer, or until meat is tender. Remove meat and vegetables to serving platter. Place dutch oven on range and pour off all but 1/4 cup of juice, reserving remainder. Add flour and stir over low heat until well blended. Cook 1 minute longer. Measure 1 1/2 cups reserved pan juice (add water if necessary to make 1 1/2 cups), add remaining 1/2 cup Madeira and add the 2 cups of liquid slowly to flour mixture, stirring constantly, until slightly thickened. Taste and adjust seasoning. Serve with brisket.

6 servings

BEEF BIRDS

Cut steak into 3×4-inch slices and pound to about 1/8 inch thick. Combine nuts, mushrooms, cheese, parsley, garlic powder, salt, and water. Spread filling on strips of meat. Roll and tie with string or secure with skewers. Place beef birds in a greased 8-inch square baking pan. Combine wine, flour, and tomato paste, and pour over birds. Bake, covered, in convection oven on rack position 2 at 350° for 1 hour, or until the steak is tender. Birds may be uncovered for the last 15 minutes for a darker brown color.

6 servings

- 2 pounds round steak, 1/2 inch thick
- 1/2 cup pine nuts
- 1/4 cup sliced mushrooms
- 1 cup grated Parmesan cheese
- 1/4 cup chopped parsley or 1 tablespoon dry parsley
- 1/2 teaspoon garlic powder
- 1 teaspoon salt
- 1/2 cup hot water
- 1/2 cup dry red wine
- 1 tablespoon all-purpose flour
- 1 tablespoon tomato paste

SAUSAGE-STUFFED FLANK STEAK

Pound the steak very thin. Sauté sausage, onion, carrot, garlic, apple, and green pepper until tender; drain. Add remaining ingredients except barbecue sauce and mix thoroughly. Spread on steak. Roll, starting from the short end, and secure with skewers or string. Place in a greased 9×13-inch roasting pan, seam side up. Drizzle with barbecue sauce. Bake in convection oven on rack position 2 at 350° for 1 hour, or until steak is tender.

8 servings

- 2 pounds flank steak
- 1/2 pound mild (sweet) Italian sausage
- 1/4 cup chopped onion
- 1/2 cup minced carrot
- 2 cloves garlic, minced
- 1 medium apple, peeled, cored, and chopped
- 1/3 cup diced green pepper
- 1 cup seasoned bread stuffing mix
- 1 egg
- 1/2 cup chopped parsley or 2 tablespoons dry parsley
- 1/4 cup red wine
- 2/3 cup Barbecue Sauce (page 41)

MEAT LOAF WITH LOUISIANA CREOLE SAUCE

Combine all ingredients and mix thoroughly with hands. Form mixture into a slightly flattened round loaf and place on a rack in a shallow 10-inch baking dish. Preheat convection oven to 400°. Place baking dish on rack position 2 and bake for 15 minutes. Reduce temperature to 350° and continue baking 30 minutes longer. Remove from rack with a spatula, allow to drain, and place on serving platter. Serve with Louisiana Creole Sauce.

Note: You can put the Louisiana Creole Sauce into the oven when the meat loaf goes in; cover it loosely with foil until the oven temperature is reduced to 350°.

4 to 6 servings

1 1/2 pounds lean ground beef
1 medium-size onion, finely chopped
1/2 cup seasoned dry bread crumbs
1 tablespoon finely chopped parsley or 1 teaspoon dry parsley
1 teaspoon oregano
1/2 teaspoon thyme
1/2 teaspoon marjoram
2 teaspoons prepared mustard
1 tablespoon Worcestershire sauce
1/2 cup tomato sauce
2 eggs, lightly beaten
Salt and pepper

Louisiana Creole Sauce

Heat oil in large skillet, add onions, green pepper, and celery and sauté until onion is transparent. Add mushrooms, parsley, and garlic, and cook until mushrooms are tender. Add stock, tomato paste, tomatoes, salt, and pepper. Crush the tomatoes with the side of a spoon and stir until all ingredients are well combined. Add crushed red pepper and stir. Pour contents of skillet into a 3-quart casserole. Bake in convection oven on rack position 2 at 350° for 45 minutes, stirring once or twice. Serve with meat loaf or fish.

6 cups

Nice to know: This sauce freezes very well. Use half and freeze the remainder to use at another time.

3 tablespoons vegetable oil
2 medium-size onions, finely chopped
1 large green pepper, finely chopped
4 stalks celery, finely chopped
12 ounces mushrooms, sliced
3 tablespoons finely chopped parsley or 1 tablespoon dry parsley
3 cloves garlic, minced, or 1 tablespoon minced dry garlic
1 3/4 cup beef stock
1 can (6 ounces) tomato paste
1 can (28 ounces) tomatoes
Salt and pepper
1/4 to 1/2 teaspoon crushed red pepper

Meat Loaf with Louisiana Creole Sauce
French Bread (page 147)

CALIFORNIA POT ROAST

1   boneless chuck roast
      (3 pounds)
1/2 cup vegetable oil
1/4 cup lemon juice
1 1/2 teaspoons paprika
2   tablespoons
      Worcestershire sauce
    Dash hot pepper sauce
2   tablespoons white
      vinegar
2   teaspoons salt
2   teaspoons sugar
2   cloves garlic,
      crushed

Trim all excess fat from roast. Place in 13×9×2-inch pan. Combine all other ingredients and mix thoroughly. Pour over roast and refrigerate, tightly covered, 6 hours or longer. Bake, uncovered, in convection oven on rack position 2 at 350° for 2 hours, or until internal temperature reaches 170°. Add 1 cup water to drippings after 1 hour of roasting. Remove roast and keep warm while making gravy.

Slowly stir a mixture of 2 tablespoons flour dissolved in 1/2 cup cold water into roast drippings. Stir until thickened over medium heat. Taste for seasoning.

6 to 8 servings

STUFFED MEAT LOAF

Meat mixture

1/2 pound ground beef
1/2 pound ground veal
1/2 pound ground pork
1/3 cup milk
1   egg
2   tablespoons
      minced onion
1/2 teaspoon salt
1/4 teaspoon pepper
1/4 teaspoon sage

Stuffing

1   cup dry bread crumbs
2   tablespoons
      minced onion
1/2 teaspoon salt
1/2 teaspoon pepper
1   cup chopped celery
1/2 cup dry red wine
3/4 cup chopped walnuts

1   cup tomato sauce

Thoroughly combine ingredients for meat loaf; roll flat on waxed paper into a 12×15-inch rectangle. Combine ingredients for stuffing and spread evenly on the meat. Roll up meat starting at the short edge; seal edges and ends. Place in a shallow 11×14-inch roasting pan and pour the tomato sauce over the meat loaf. Bake in convection oven on rack position 2 at 325° for 1 hour and 15 minutes. Serve hot with salad and dinner rolls.

6 servings

BEEF WELLINGTON

Preheat convection oven to 475°. Bake tenderloin in a greased 9×13-inch pan on rack position 2 for 15 minutes. Cool thoroughly. Mix together mushrooms, livers, lemon juice, salt, and pepper; set aside. Blend together flour, salt, and margarine. Stir in egg yolks and water. Roll out on a lightly floured surface into an 18×20-inch rectangle. Reserve a small portion of dough for decorating top. Spread the mushroom-liver pâté evenly on the dough. Lay the tenderloin on the pastry. Fold pastry over meat and seal ends and sides. Return to baking pan, seam side down, and decorate with designs cut out of reserved dough. Refrigerate 2 hours before baking. Bake on rack position 2 at 375° for 35 to 50 minutes, or until pastry is brown and the internal temperature of the meat reaches 140° for rare or 160° for medium.

Note: A food processor makes quick work of preparing the pâté.

6 to 8 servings

1 beef tenderloin (3 pounds), trimmed
1 cup finely chopped mushrooms
1 cup cooked finely chopped chicken livers
1 teaspoon lemon juice
1/2 teaspoon salt
1/4 teaspoon pepper

Pastry

4 cups all-purpose flour
1/2 teaspoon salt
1 cup margarine or butter
3 egg yolks
1 cup very cold water

HEARTY BEEF CASSEROLE

Place meat, mushrooms, onion, and celery in a shallow 2 1/2-quart casserole. Combine tomato sauce, sour cream, Worcestershire, salt, and pepper. Pour over meat and stir lightly to mix well. Cover and bake in convection oven on rack position 2 at 325° for 1 hour. Uncover casserole, stir, and bake 1 hour and 15 minutes longer, or until meat is fork tender. Serve over rice or noodles.

Note: This dish freezes very well; make two batches and put one away for a no-work meal later.

8 servings

2 1/2 pounds boneless beef chuck, in 1 1/2-inch cubes
8 ounces mushrooms, quartered
1 medium-size onion, chopped
1/2 cup chopped celery
1 can (15 ounces) herbed tomato sauce or 1 can (15 ounces) tomato sauce plus 1/2 teaspoon each thyme and oregano
1 cup dairy sour cream
1 tablespoon Worcestershire sauce
1 teaspoon salt
1/4 teaspoon pepper

OVEN CHILI

1 pound lean
    ground beef
1 medium-size onion,
    chopped
1/3 cup chopped
    green pepper
1 can (29 ounces)
    tomato sauce
1 can (30 ounces) red
    kidney beans,
    drained and rinsed
1/2 teaspoon salt
1 to 2 teaspoons
    chili powder

Preheat convection oven to 400°. Crumble ground beef evenly over the bottom of a shallow 11×14-inch baking pan. Brown on rack position 3 for 10 minutes; stir twice to break up meat. Reduce heat to 325°. Add all other ingredients to pan and stir well. Bake on rack position 2 for 1 hour and 45 minutes. Serve hot with corn bread or crackers. This chili is thick and delicious.

Note: This recipe can be doubled easily.

6 servings

OVEN BEEF BOURGUIGNON

6 slices bacon
2 pounds boneless
    round steak
1/2 cup all-purpose flour
1 1/2 teaspoons salt,
    divided
1/2 teaspoon pepper
2 cloves garlic, minced,
    or 2 teaspoons
    minced dry garlic
2 tablespoons brandy
12 small whole mushrooms
12 1-inch onions
1 cup beef stock or
    1 can (10 1/2 ounces)
    beef bouillon
2 cups dry red wine,
    divided
3 carrots, sliced
3 peppercorns, crushed
1/4 teaspoon clove
1 bay leaf
1 tablespoon chervil
1/4 teaspoon marjoram
1/4 teaspoon thyme

Cut bacon into 1-inch pieces. Fry until crisp in a large skillet over medium heat. Remove bacon and put into a 9×13-inch baking pan. Cut meat into 1-inch cubes and roll in flour, 1 teaspoon salt, and pepper. Brown the meat in bacon drippings with garlic. Add brandy and ignite. Stir until flames go out. Remove meat and combine with bacon. Slightly brown mushrooms and onions in bacon fat (add a little butter or oil to skillet if necessary) and add to meat mixture. Add beef bouillon and 1 cup wine to skillet; bring to boil over high heat; stir to loosen all brown bits from pan. Pour over meat mixture. Add remaining cup wine and all other ingredients; mix. Bake in convection oven on rack position 2 at 350° for 1 hour, or until meat is tender and vegetables cooked. Serve hot with boiled potatoes or over wide noodles.

6 to 8 servings

BEEF JERKY

1 to 1 1/2 pounds round
   or flank steak
1 teaspoon salt

Remove all visible fat from the steak. Partially freeze it for ease in slicing into 1/8-inch thick strips. Cut each strip into 4-inch pieces. Toss meat with salt to distribute it evenly. Place on a rack on a large baking sheet. Bake in convection oven on rack position 2 at 175° for 8 to 10 hours, until meat is quite dry and crisp. Pat dry with paper towels and cool. Store at room temperature in a very tightly covered container.

4 to 5 servings

BEEF AND SPINACH PIE

Pastry for 1
   single-crust 9-inch
   pie, unbaked
1 cup chopped onion
1 1/2 tablespoons butter
   or margarine
1/2 pound lean
   ground beef
1 package (10 ounces)
   frozen chopped
   spinach, thawed
   and drained
1/2 cup grated sharp
   Cheddar cheese
3/4 teaspoon salt
1/4 teaspoon pepper
1/8 teaspoon nutmeg
2 eggs
1 cup light cream

Bake pie shell in convection oven on rack position 2 at 400° for 15 minutes; cool. In skillet cook onion in butter until transparent. Break up ground beef and add to onion. Sauté, stirring occasionally, until beef loses its pink color; do not brown. Distribute onion, beef, spinach, and cheese in pie shell. Combine salt, pepper, nutmeg, eggs, and cream. Pour carefully into pie shell. Bake in convection oven on rack position 2 at 375° for 30 minutes, or until set in center. Let stand 5 minutes before serving.

6 servings

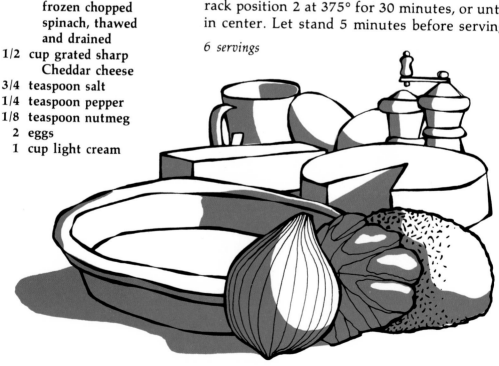

CROWN ROAST OF PORK WITH FRUIT DRESSING

Season roast with salt and pepper and cover any exposed bone with foil to prevent burning. Place meat, bone ends up, on a rack in a shallow 11×14-inch roasting pan. Bake in convection oven on rack position 1 at 325° for 2 hours. Baste occasionally with pan drippings.

Sauté the onion and celery in butter until transparent. Combine with all other ingredients. Pack dressing in center of roast and cover with foil. Continue baking 1 hour and 30 minutes, or until internal temperature reaches 170°. Remove all foil from roast before serving. Decorate bone ends with paper frills.

If there is more dressing than the roast will hold, place excess in a small greased casserole and bake, covered, at 325° for 30 minutes along with the roast. If you cook the dressing separately use rack position 2.

8 to 10 servings

1 crown roast of pork (about 7 pounds)
1/2 teaspoon salt
1/4 teaspoon pepper
2 medium-size onions, chopped
1 cup chopped celery
2 tablespoons butter
1 cup dry bread crumbs
2 cups cooked rice
1/2 teaspoon poultry seasoning
2 cans (8 ounces each) pineapple chunks, drained
1 cup mandarin orange segments, drained
1/2 cup raisins
1/4 cup slivered almonds

SWEET SOUR PORK ROAST

Rub an 8×11-inch roasting pan with a small piece of fat from the roast (makes clean-up easier). Place roast, fat side up (resting on bones) in pan. Combine cornstarch, sugar, salt, paprika, and parsley in saucepan. Stir in vinegar and 1 cup water. Bring to a boil over high heat. Boil, stirring constantly, until thickened. Pour over roast. Bake in convection oven on rack position 2 at 300° for 2 hours, or until internal temperature reaches 170°. Baste with pan drippings occasionally. Slice and serve hot.

6 servings

1 loin pork roast (3 pounds)
4 tablespoons cornstarch
2 cups sugar
1 teaspoon salt
2 teaspoons paprika
2 teaspoons minced parsley
1 cup cider vinegar

HAM MOLD

2 pounds ground smoked
    ham (about 4 cups)
2/3 cup milk
4 eggs, beaten
1/2 teaspoon dry mustard
1/4 teaspoon
    Worcestershire sauce

Combine all ingredients and press into a 1-quart ring mold. Bake in convection oven on rack position 2 at 375° for 1 hour. Place cookie sheet or foil square under ring mold to catch possible spills. Unmold on round serving platter.

Note: Ham mold can be presented surrounded by sweet potatoes with a hot green vegetable in center of mold.

6 servings

Nice to know: A pleasant oven meal would be Ham Mold, Winter Squash and Apple Purée (page 136), and Snow Peas (page 123).

HAM LOAF WITH MUSTARD SAUCE

1 1/2 pounds ground ham
1 1/2 pounds ground
    round steak
1 can (6 ounces) tomato
    paste, divided
1 egg
1 cup dry bread crumbs
1/2 cup milk
1/2 teaspoon paprika
1/4 teaspoon salt

Combine all ingredients using 4 tablespoons of the tomato paste. Pack tightly into a greased 9×5×3-inch loaf pan. Bake in convection oven on rack position 2 at 325° for 1 hour and 25 minutes, or until loaf is thoroughly browned. Drain any fat and unmold on serving platter. Serve with Hot Mustard Sauce.

8 servings

Hot Mustard Sauce

Remaining tomato
    paste (about 1/2 cup)
1/2 cup spicy brown mustard
1/2 cup cider vinegar
1/2 cup sugar
4 tablespoons butter
    or margarine
3 eggs

Combine all ingredients and cook in double boiler over medium heat, stirring constantly until sauce is thick. Sauce may be reheated in double boiler.

2 cups

VEGETABLE STUFFED PORK CHOPS

Combine corn, green pepper, celery, bread crumbs, and 1/2 cup water. Cut a large pocket in each pork chop and fill with stuffing. Fasten closure with skewers or lace with poultry string. Mix flour, salt, and pepper. Roll each pork chop in mixture. Place in greased 13×9-inch pan; pour tomatoes over chops. Place 1 apple and 1 green pepper ring on each pork chop. Bake, covered, in convection oven at 350° for 1 hour. Uncover and bake an additional 15 minutes or until chops are brown. Serve hot.

6 servings

- 1 package (10 ounces) frozen corn, thawed
- 1/4 cup chopped green pepper
- 1/2 cup chopped celery
- 1 cup dry bread crumbs
- 6 pork chops, 2 inches thick
- 1/2 cup flour
- 1/2 teaspoon salt
- 1/4 teaspoon pepper
- 1 can (28 ounces) whole tomatoes
- 1 apple, cored and cut into 6 rings
- 1 green pepper, cored and cut into 6 rings

POLYNESIAN PORK

Cut pork into 2×1/2-inch strips; sprinkle with paprika. Place meat, green pepper, onion, and pineapple in the bottom of a greased 1 1/2-quart casserole. Combine remaining ingredients and pour over meat. Bake in convection oven on rack position 2 at 300° for 1 hour and 30 minutes, or until pork is tender. Serve hot over rice.

4 to 6 servings

- 1 pound fresh pork shoulder
- 1 teaspoon paprika
- 1/2 cup chopped green pepper
- 1 small onion, sliced thin
- 1 can (15 1/4 ounces) pineapple tidbits, drained, syrup reserved
- 3 tablespoons brown sugar
- 1/4 cup instant dry milk
- 2 tablespoons cornstarch
- 1/2 teaspoon salt
- 1 tablespoon soy sauce
- 1/4 cup cider vinegar
- 1 teaspoon Worcestershire sauce

NEW ENGLAND GLAZED HAM

1 fully-cooked shank
   end of ham
   (10 to 12 pounds)
1 jar (14 ounces)
   cranberry-orange
   relish
1/2 cup orange juice
1/4 cup brown sugar
1/4 teaspoon cinnamon
1/8 teaspoon clove
1/8 teaspoon salt
   Whole cloves
   (optional)

Place the ham on a rack in an 11×14-inch baking pan. Start baking in convection oven on rack position 1 at 300°. Meanwhile, heat the relish, orange juice, brown sugar, cinnamon, and clove in a small saucepan. When the internal temperature of the ham reaches 120° (about 2 hours), remove from oven. Take off skin and trim fat to an even layer about 1/4 inch thick. Score fat and stud each diamond with a whole clove. Brush with cranberry-orange mixture and return ham to oven. Continue baking, basting often, until internal temperature of the ham reaches 140° (about another hour). Serve hot or cold. Ham may be garnished with roasted apples or with orange halves decorated with cranberry relish.

18 to 20 servings

Roasted Apples

10 to 12 medium-size
   McIntosh apples
1/2 cup butter, melted
   Cinnamon (optional)

Halve unpeeled apples lengthwise and remove core. Arrange on rack around the ham and brush with melted butter. Bake in convection oven with ham at 300° for 30 to 45 minutes. The apples should be very tender and slightly puffed. Sprinkle with cinnamon or brush lightly when done with cranberry glaze from ham.

18 to 20 servings

SPANISH PORK CHOPS

2 cups long-grained rice
1/2 cup chopped onion
1/2 cup chopped
   green pepper
1 bay leaf, crumbled
6 loin pork chops,
   1 inch thick
1 can (28 ounces)
   whole tomatoes

Sprinkle rice over bottom of 9×13-inch pan. Add onion, green pepper, and bay leaf. Lay pork chops on rice and vegetables. Pour tomatoes and 2 cups water over all. Bake, covered with foil, in convection oven on rack position 2 at 375° for 1 hour and 30 minutes. Uncover and bake an additional 30 minutes.

6 servings

New England Glazed Ham

VEAL CORDON BLEU

4 6-ounce veal cutlets
4 slices Swiss cheese
4 slices ham
1/2 cup dry bread crumbs
1 egg, beaten
Lemon wedges

Pound the veal cutlets 1/4 inch thick. Place a slice of cheese and a slice of ham on each cutlet. Roll up and dip into bread crumbs and then into egg and then into crumbs again. Place seam side down in a greased 6-inch square pan. Bake in convection oven on rack position 2 at 325° for 45 minutes, or until meat is done and cheese is melted. Serve garnished with wedges of lemon.

4 servings

CREAMED VEAL AND MUSHROOMS

1 pound veal leg round steak, thinly sliced
Salt and pepper
2 tablespoons butter
1 tablespoon olive oil
1 onion, thinly sliced
1/2 pound mushrooms, sliced
1/2 cup dry sherry
1/2 cup half-and-half
1/2 teaspoon Worcestershire sauce

Season veal with salt and pepper; melt butter with oil in a large skillet, add veal, and brown on both sides (about 1 minute per side). Remove to a round 2-quart baking dish. In same skillet, sauté onion and mushrooms until tender; spoon over veal. To skillet add sherry, half-and-half, Worcestershire, and more salt and pepper to taste and heat through. Pour over veal and bake in convection oven on rack position 2 at 325° for 20 minutes, or until veal is tender.

4 servings

Nice to know: Creamed Veal and Mushrooms, Zucchini Bread (page 143), and Coconut Ginger Cake (page 157) make an easy meal-in-the-oven.

BAKED VEAL STEW

1 1/2 pounds veal shoulder round bone steak
1/4 cup chopped onion
1/4 cup chopped green pepper
1 medium-size potato, peeled and chopped
1/4 cup barley
1/2 teaspoon salt
1/4 teaspoon pepper
1 bay leaf, crumbled
1/2 cup dry white wine

Cut veal into 1-inch cubes. Combine all ingredients with 1/2 cup water in greased 1-quart casserole. Bake, covered, in convection oven on rack position 2 at 325° for 1 hour and 15 minutes, or until meat and vegetables are tender. Serve hot with green salad.

Note: Make this stew without the potato for freezing. Serve with baked or boiled potatoes.

4 servings

VEAL CUTLETS WITH ONIONS AND CHEESE

Sauté onions in 2 tablespoons of the butter until transparent. Place half the onions in bottom of an 11×14×2-inch baking pan. Sprinkle cutlets with salt and pepper; place on top of onions and cover with remaining onion. Mix cheese with bread crumbs and sprinkle over onions. Dot with remaining butter. Combine wine and broth; pour carefully over top. Bake in convection oven on rack position 2 at 325° for 1 hour, or until cutlets are fork tender. Serve hot.

Note: For an interesting variation, use plain dry bread crumbs and grated Gruyère cheese.

6 servings

- 3 medium-size onions, sliced
- 6 tablespoons butter or margarine, divided
- 6 veal cutlets (about 1 1/2 pounds)
  Salt
  Pepper
- 1 cup grated Cheddar cheese
- 1/2 cup seasoned bread crumbs
- 1/2 cup dry white wine
- 3/4 cup chicken broth

EUROPEAN VEAL PIE

Cut veal into 1/2-inch cubes. Combine veal, onion, mushrooms, and seasonings in small bowl and mix. Blend together flour, shortening, and salt until fine crumb texture; stir in 1/2 cup iced water. Roll out half the dough on lightly floured surface to fit 8-inch pie plate; crimp edge. Pour in veal mixture. Roll out remaining dough and cut into 8 circles; overlap circles and place around pie top. Bake in convection oven on rack position 2 at 325° for 1 hour and 30 minutes, or until veal is tender and crust is brown. Cut in wedges and serve hot.

4 servings

- 1 pound veal stew meat
- 1/2 cup chopped onion
- 1 cup chopped mushrooms
- 1/4 teaspoon thyme
- 1/4 teaspoon marjoram
- 1/2 teaspoon salt
- 1/4 teaspoon pepper
- 2 cups all-purpose flour
- 1 cup shortening
- 1/2 teaspoon salt
- 1/2 cup iced water

VEAL PROVENÇALE

Mix together meat, onion, bread crumbs, salt, pepper, mint, basil, and egg. Wash and trim ends of squash; cut in half lengthwise and remove seeds. Divide meat mixture between halves of squash and sprinkle with cheese. Place squash in a greased 9×13-inch pan and bake in convection oven on rack position 2 at 350° for 45 minutes. Serve hot with spaghetti dressed with butter and more cheese.

6 to 8 servings

- 1 1/2 pounds ground veal
- 1/4 cup chopped onion
- 1/2 cup dry bread crumbs
  Salt and pepper
- 1/4 teaspoon mint
- 1/4 teaspoon basil
- 1 egg
- 1 large or 4 small summer squash
- 1/2 cup grated Parmesan cheese

MINTED LEG OF LAMB

1 leg of lamb
(5 pounds)
1/2 teaspoon salt
1 or 2 cloves garlic,
slivered
3/4 cup mint jelly
1/2 cup cider vinegar
1/4 cup firmly packed
brown sugar
1/4 cup sugar
1 tablespoon butter
1 teaspoon grated
lemon rind
1 teaspoon grated
orange rind

Score lamb fat in diamond pattern; sprinkle with salt; stud with garlic slivers. In a small saucepan, combine jelly, vinegar, brown sugar, sugar, butter, lemon rind, and orange rind; heat until smooth. Let cool; pour over lamb and let stand 1/2 hour at room temperature. Roast in convection oven on rack position 2 at 300°, basting occasionally, for about 1 hour and 45 minutes for rare (140°), 2 hours for medium (160°), and 2 hours and 15 minutes for well done (170°). Remove from roasting pan and allow meat to rest 15 minutes before carving. Pour juices from pan into a small saucepan. Skim off fat, heat thoroughly, and serve with lamb.

6 servings

LAMB A L'APRICOT

1 package (6 ounces)
dried apricots
1/4 cup minced onion
1 tablespoon
lemon juice
1/2 teaspoon allspice
1/4 teaspoon pepper
1 cup cooked rice
1 egg
1 boned lamb shoulder
(about 2 1/2 pounds)

Place apricots in saucepan and cover with water. Bring to a boil on high heat and boil 5 minutes; drain, cool, and finely chop. (The cutting blade of a food processor works well.) Combine apricots with remaining ingredients except the lamb. Fill lamb pocket with apricot mixture and tie with string or secure with skewers. Place in a 9-inch baking dish. Bake, covered, in convection oven on rack position 2 at 350° for 1 hour and 20 minutes, or until thermometer inserted in meat reaches 160° for medium. Remove skewers or string before serving.

Note: The lamb pocket is formed when the butcher removes the shoulder bone.

6 servings

LAMB LOAF

Combine all ingredients except bacon and form into loaf. Place in loaf pan and top with bacon slices. Bake in convection oven on rack position 2 at 350° for 1 hour. Serve hot with green salad and parsleyed new potatoes.

Note: Snip parsley with kitchen shears to mince quickly.

8 servings

Nice to know: Lamb Loaf, Elegant Corn Casserole (page 135), and Peach Crisp (page 162) bake at the same time for an energy-economical oven meal.

2 pounds ground lamb
1 cup dry bread crumbs
1/2 cup minced onion
1/4 cup minced parsley or
    1 tablespoon dry
    parsley
1 clove garlic, minced
1/2 teaspoon
    Worcestershire sauce
1 1/2 teaspoons salt
1 teaspoon dry mustard
2 eggs
3 slices bacon

NEW DELHI CURRY

Cut meat into 1 1/2-inch cubes. Mix lamb, onions, and almonds with spices and place in a greased 8-inch square casserole. Combine yogurt and tomato sauce and pour over meat. Bake in convection oven on rack position 2 at 350° for 1 hour, or until meat is tender. Serve hot with rice.

6 servings

2 pounds lamb stew meat
2 medium-size onions,
    chopped
1/2 cup slivered
    almonds
1/2 teaspoon ginger
1 1/2 teaspoons salt
1/2 teaspoon chili powder
1/2 teaspoon curry powder
3/4 cup plain yogurt
1 can (15 ounces)
    tomato sauce with
    tomato bits

CHICKEN DIJONNAISE

Dry the chicken pieces thoroughly and sprinkle all over with flour, shaking off any excess. In a large skillet, melt 2 tablespoons of the butter with 1 tablespoon of oil. Add as many pieces of chicken as will fit without crowding and brown 2 to 3 minutes per side. Remove browned pieces to a plate and brown remaining chicken, adding an additional 2 tablespoons of butter and 1 of oil to skillet. Arrange browned chicken in an 11×13×2-inch gratin or baking dish and sprinkle with salt and pepper.

Prepare sauce: Melt butter in a saucepan over moderate heat. Blend in flour and cook 2 minutes, stirring often. Add broth and wine and bring to a boil, stirring until sauce is thickened and smooth. Stir in the mustard, tarragon, cream, and pepper, and simmer 5 minutes, stirring occasionally. Remove from heat and stir in 1/2 cup of the cheese. Sauce can be made several hours ahead of time, covered, and refrigerated. Reheat before assembling dish. About 20 minutes before serving, pour heated sauce over chicken. Combine remaining cheese with crumbs and sprinkle over chicken. Bake in convection oven on rack position 2 at 400° for 15 minutes until golden brown. Serve from pan with buttered rice, spooning some of the sauce over each serving.

8 servings

4 chicken breasts,
   halved
   All-purpose flour
4 tablespoons unsalted
   butter or margarine,
   divided
2 tablespoons vegetable
   oil, divided
   Salt and pepper

Dijonnaise Sauce

3 tablespoons butter
4 tablespoons
   all-purpose flour
1 cup chicken broth
1/2 cup dry white wine
1 tablespoon Dijon
   mustard
1 teaspoon tarragon
1 cup heavy cream
1/4 teaspoon pepper
1 cup coarsely grated
   Swiss cheese,
   divided
1/4 cup fine dry
   bread crumbs

APRICOT STUFFED CHICKEN

Roughly chop apricots and cook according to package directions. Wash and carefully dry chicken inside and out. Trim any visible fat from the cavity and discard. Combine all remaining ingredients for stuffing; moisten with about 1 cup water or chicken stock and mix well. Fill the chicken cavity. Tie wings to body and legs together. Place on a rack in a shallow roasting pan and bake in convection oven on rack position 2 at 275° for 2 to 2 1/2 hours, or until internal temperature reaches 185° in thigh or breast.

6 servings

Chicken Dijonnaise
French Dinner Rolls (page 147)

1 package (6 ounces)
   dried apricots
1 roasting chicken
   (4 to 6 pounds)
1 cup chopped celery
2 tablespoons
   minced onion
2 teaspoons lemon juice
3 cups dry 1/2-inch
   bread cubes
1 teaspoon salt
1/8 teaspoon pepper
1/2 teaspoon paprika

CORNISH HENS WITH SAUSAGE-RICE STUFFING

4 fresh or frozen
  Cornish hens
  (about 1 pound each),
  thawed
1/2 pound mild (sweet)
  Italian sausage,
  casings removed
1 cup diced onion
2 cups cooked rice
  (cooked in chicken
  broth)
1/4 cup grated Parmesan
  cheese
1/4 cup chopped parsley or
  1 tablespoon dry
  parsley
1/2 teaspoon pepper
1 stick (1/2 cup)
  unsalted butter,
  softened
  Watercress

Rinse hens and pat dry with a paper towel. In a large skillet, sauté sausage over moderate heat, stirring often and breaking it up with the side of a spoon. When sausage loses most of its pink color, add onion and sauté until onion is soft. Add remaining ingredients except butter and watercress and toss to blend. Sprinkle insides of hens with salt and additional pepper. Fill the cavity of each bird with about 3/4 cup of stuffing. Tuck wings under hens and tie legs tightly together. Arrange hens breast side up in a large shallow roasting pan and rub each with 1 tablespoon of the butter. Roast in convection oven on rack position 2 at 350° for 1 hour, basting several times with pan drippings and remaining butter. To serve, remove trussing strings and arrange hens on a serving platter. Garnish with watercress. Reheat pan drippings and serve separately.

Note: This stuffing is also very good for turkey or pheasant.

4 servings

HERB BAKED CHICKEN

2 tablespoons chopped
  chives
1 tablespoon
  minced parsley
1/2 teaspoon
  minced tarragon
1/4 teaspoon
  poultry seasoning
1/2 cup butter or
  margarine, softened
3 broiling chickens
  (1 1/2 to 2 pounds
  each), split
  lengthwise
  White pepper
  Salt

Add herbs and seasoning to butter; blend well. Wash and pat chicken dry. Gently loosen skin of broilers so the herb butter can be spread under the skin. Start at the breast side to make pocket. Arrange broiler halves, not touching, on 2 10×15×1-inch baking sheets, skin side up. Season with salt and pepper. Bake in convection oven on rack positions 1 and 3 at 400° for 40 to 45 minutes, or until crisply brown. After 20 minutes rotate baking sheets. Baste with drippings occasionally.

Note: The fresh herbs give this dish its piquancy and character. Make it when fresh herbs are available in abundance.

6 servings

Stuffed Cornish Hens

CHICKEN DIVINE

4 chicken breasts,
    boned, skinned,
    and halved
4 large stalks broccoli,
    cooked and drained
4 tablespoons butter
4 tablespoons
    all-purpose flour
1 1/2 cups chicken stock or
    1 (10 3/4 ounces)
    can chicken broth
1/4 cup heavy cream
1 tablespoon grated
    Parmesan cheese
1/2 teaspoon salt
1/4 teaspoon pepper
2 egg yolks,
    lightly beaten
1 tablespoon
    lemon juice
1/4 teaspoon curry powder

In a large saucepan, over medium heat, poach chicken breasts in unsalted water to cover for about 30 minutes, or until tender. Grease an attractive oven-proof 11×14-inch shallow baking dish. Split broccoli spears lengthwise and place on bottom of dish; top with halves of chicken breasts.

Melt butter in saucepan and stir in flour. Slowly stir in stock and cook until thickened. Slowly add cream, cheese, salt, and pepper. Remove from heat. Stir some of the sauce into the egg yolks and then add the mixture to saucepan. Add lemon juice and curry powder. Taste for salt. Pour over broccoli and chicken. Bake in convection oven on rack position 2 at 325° for 25 minutes. Serve hot.

Note: The stock in which the chicken has been poached may be too fatty to use right away, but if you cook the chicken ahead, the stock can be cooled and defatted. Then it can be reduced slightly and 1 1/4 cups used to make the sauce. In any case, save the cooking broth to use in other dishes after it has been defatted.

8 servings

DEVILED TURKEY LEGS

3 turkey legs
    (about 4 1/2 pounds)
2 cups fine dry
    bread crumbs
1 teaspoon salt
1 teaspoon pepper
1/2 teaspoon cayenne
2 teaspoons dry mustard
1 cup margarine or
    butter (1/2 pound)

Rinse the turkey legs and pat dry. Combine all other ingredients except the margarine in a shallow plate. Turn on convection oven to 325°. Melt the margarine in an 11×14×2-inch pan in oven. Roll turkey legs in margarine, then in crumb mixture; place in baking pan. Bake on rack position 2 for 45 minutes to 1 hour, or until internal temperature reaches 185°. Baste with pan juices occasionally, but be careful not to disturb the crust. Cut meat off bones and serve hot or cold.

Note: Frozen turkey may be used in this recipe. Allow about 20 minutes extra cooking time.

6 servings

NEW ENGLAND TURKEY

Put turkey parts in a large saucepan; add wine and enough water to cover. Season with salt and pepper. Bring to a boil over high heat; reduce temperature and simmer, covered, for 30 minutes, or until turkey is tender. Remove from cooking liquid and cool. Reserve cooking liquid. Cut meat from bones and into bite-size pieces. Add macaroni to boiling cooking liquid and cook 10 minutes; drain. Add to turkey meat. Mix in remaining ingredients except cracker crumbs and cheese. Grease an 8×12×3-inch pan and layer turkey mixture, crumbs, and cheese. Repeat layering until all ingredients are used, ending with cheese. Bake in convection oven on rack position 2 at 350° for 25 minutes, or until cheese is melted and top is brown. Serve hot with spinach salad and rolls.

6 servings

3 pounds turkey wings
   or legs
1 cup dry white wine
   Salt and pepper
2 cups shell macaroni
1/4 cup chopped
   green pepper
1/4 cup chopped pimiento
1 can (4 ounces) button
   mushrooms, drained
1 can (10 1/2 ounces)
   cream of chicken
   soup, undiluted
2 tablespoons sesame seed
1/2 teaspoon
   Worcestershire sauce
1 cup cheese-cracker
   crumbs
1 cup grated sharp
   Cheddar cheese

CHINESE BARBECUED CHICKEN

Blend marinade ingredients in a large shallow roasting pan. Add chicken parts, cover, and marinate in refrigerator 4 to 24 hours. Combine Barbecue Sauce ingredients in a saucepan and bring to a boil, stirring often. Reduce heat to low and simmer 5 minutes, stirring often. Set sauce aside until needed. If sauce is made far in advance, reheat before using. About 1 hour before serving, drain chicken and discard marinade. Pour Barbecue Sauce over chicken and coat thoroughly. Turn pieces skin side down. Place pan in convection oven on rack position 2 and bake at 350° for 25 minutes. Turn chicken, baste, and bake 20 minutes longer, removing breast pieces after 15 minutes. Serve from pan with sauce.

6 to 8 servings

Marinade

3/4 cup soy sauce
3/4 cup dry sherry
1 teaspoon
   minced garlic
1 tablespoon minced
   fresh gingerroot or
   1 teaspoon ground
   ginger
2 broiler-fryer chickens
   (3 1/2-pounds each)
   cut in serving pieces

Barbecue Sauce

1 1/2 cups catsup
1/2 cup firmly packed
   dark brown sugar
1/4 cup Worcestershire
   sauce

CRISP ROAST DUCK WITH SWEET AND SOUR CURRY SAUCE

Remove and discard giblets and neck from inside duckling. Rinse bird inside and out and pat dry. Rub duck skin all over with cut sides of garlic clove. Sprinkle inside of duck with lemon juice, salt, and pepper and tuck the lemon half and remaining garlic inside. Prick skin. Place the duck on a rack in a roasting pan and roast in convection oven on rack position 2 at 350° for 2 hours, pricking skin every 30 minutes. Meanwhile, prepare sauce: Combine mustard, honey, and curry powder in a small saucepan and stir to blend. Bring to a boil, stirring often. Reduce heat to low and simmer 2 minutes, stirring to prevent sauce from sticking. Reheat sauce just before serving. To serve, cut duck in quarters with poultry shears and serve with sauce for dipping.

Note: To roast a second duck, place both birds on a large rack over a roasting pan leaving several inches between them to allow air to circulate. Roast as above. Double sauce recipe.

2 to 3 servings

1 fresh or frozen duckling, thawed (4- to 5-pounds)
1 large clove garlic, split
1/2 lemon
Salt
Pepper
1/2 cup prepared mustard
1/2 cup honey
1 tablespoon curry powder

CHICKEN BREASTS PERSILLADE

Rinse chicken and pat dry. Place chicken between sheets of waxed paper and pound 1/4 inch thick. Sprinkle lightly with salt and pepper. Turn on convection oven to 425°. Melt butter in a 15×10×1-inch baking sheet. Place crumbs, garlic, basil, parsley, and 1/2 teaspoon salt on a large plate and toss to blend. Dip each piece of chicken in butter, then in crumbs. Arrange on baking sheet. Bake on rack position 3 for 10 minutes, until crumbs are lightly browned. Serve with lemon wedges.

Note: This recipe is delicious for appetizers; cut meat into 1-inch squares before baking and serve with cocktail picks.

4 to 6 servings

3 boneless chicken breasts, skinned and halved
Salt
Pepper
1/2 cup (1 1/4-pound stick) unsalted butter or margarine
1 1/2 cups fine dry bread crumbs
1 clove garlic, minced
1 1/2 teaspoons basil
1/4 cup finely chopped parsley
Lemon wedges

Crisp Roast Duck with Sweet and Sour Curry Sauce

SEAFOOD

BAKED BASS WITH CORN BREAD STUFFING

1 4- to 5-pound fish,
    such as striped
    bass, sea bass, or
    sea trout, cleaned
    and dressed for
    stuffing, or 2 or 3
    smaller whole fish
   Salt and pepper
1/2 cup butter or
    margarine, divided
1/2 cup diced onion
1/2 cup diced celery
1/2 cup diced green pepper
3 cups crumbled
    corn bread
1 cup clam broth
1/2 cup dry white wine

Sprinkle inside of fish with salt and pepper and refrigerate while preparing stuffing. In a large skillet, melt half the butter over moderate heat. Add the onion, celery, and green pepper; sauté 5 minutes, stirring often, until onion is soft. Add the corn bread and sprinkle with 1/2 teaspoon salt and 1/4 teaspoon pepper; toss to blend. Place the fish in an 11×14×2-inch pan and fill the cavity with the stuffing. It is not necessary to sew or truss. Brush the top of the fish with the remaining butter and pour the clam broth and wine around, not over, the fish. Bake, uncovered, in convection oven on rack position 2 at 400° for 40 minutes, basting occasionally, until stuffing and top of fish are lightly browned.

6 to 8 servings

JAMAICAN CURRIED COD LOAF

2 cups flaked cooked cod
    or any lean white fish
1 cup fresh bread crumbs
1/2 cup chopped onion
2 tablespoons chopped
    parsley or 2 teaspoons
    dry parsley
3 eggs, separated
3 tablespoons melted
    butter or margarine
2 tablespoons lemon
    or lime juice
1/4 teaspoon hot
    pepper sauce
1/2 teaspoon salt

In a large bowl, combine fish with bread crumbs, onion, and parsley. Beat egg yolks with melted butter, lemon juice, hot pepper sauce, and salt; toss lightly with fish mixture. Beat the egg whites until soft peaks form; fold into fish mixture. Pour into deep, buttered 1-quart casserole and bake in convection oven at 350° on rack position 2 for 30 to 35 minutes, or until top is golden and a skewer inserted in the center comes out moist but clean. Serve from casserole; top each serving with Curry Lemon Butter.

6 servings

5 tablespoons butter
1 teaspoon curry powder
2 tablespoons lemon
    or lime juice

Curry Lemon Butter

In a small saucepan, melt butter over low heat; add curry powder and cook 2 minutes, stirring often. Add lemon juice and heat. Serve hot.

CRISP WALNUT SOLE

Sprinkle fillets with salt and pepper. Blend nuts with crumbs, salt, and pepper on a flat plate. Turn on convection oven to 425°. Melt butter in a 10×15×1-inch baking sheet. Roll each fish fillet in butter, then in the walnut-crumb mixture. Arrange fillets on same baking sheet, spooning any remaining butter over each fillet. Bake on rack position 3 for 10 minutes, or until crumbs are browned lightly. Serve with Lemon Caper Mayonnaise.

4 servings

1 1/2 pounds sole fillets
Salt and pepper
1 cup very finely chopped walnuts
1 cup fine dry bread crumbs
1/2 teaspoon salt
1/4 teaspoon pepper
1/2 cup butter or margarine

Lemon Caper Mayonnaise

Blend 1/2 cup mayonnaise with 1 1/2 teaspoons each of mashed, drained, capers and lemon juice.

MEDITERRANEAN BAKED FISH

Crush tomatoes and spread in the bottom of a 13×9×2-inch baking pan. Sprinkle with all but 1/4 cup of the parsley. Arrange fish fillets over parsley and sprinkle with salt and pepper. Scatter pepper and onion slices over fish and sprinkle with the garlic, dill, and more salt and pepper. Blend oil with flour and pour over fish. Bake in convection oven on rack position 2 at 350° for 35 to 40 minutes. Remove fillets to a warm serving platter, blend the lemon juice into the pan liquid and pour over the fish. Sprinkle with remaining parsley and garnish with olives. Serve with steamed potatoes or rice.

4 to 6 servings

1 can (35 ounces) tomatoes, drained
1 large or 2 small bunches parsley, chopped (about 1 cup), divided
2 pounds thick fish fillets such as scrod or any lean white fish
Salt and pepper
1 green pepper, cored, seeded, and thinly sliced
1 large onion, thinly sliced
1 teaspoon minced garlic
1 teaspoon dill, oregano, or basil
1/3 cup olive oil
1 tablespoon all-purpose flour
2 tablespoons lemon juice
Oil-cured ripe olives

FRESH CLAM QUICHE

Line a 9-inch quiche or pie pan with pastry and refrigerate while preparing filling. Cook bacon until crisp; drain and crumble. Cook onion in bacon fat until lightly browned. Preheat convection oven to 425°. Sprinkle bacon, onion, and clams in bottom of pastry-lined pan. Beat eggs with cream, clam juice, pepper, and nutmeg and pour into pan. Bake on rack position 2 for 10 minutes. Reduce temperature to 325° and bake 20 minutes longer, or until filling is set and top is golden. Let stand 10 minutes before cutting in wedges to serve.

4 to 6 servings

Pastry for
  1 single-crust
  9-inch pie, unbaked
4 slices bacon
1/2 cup diced onion
1 cup chopped fresh or canned clams, clam juice reserved
4 eggs
1 cup heavy cream
1/2 cup clam juice
1/4 teaspoon pepper
1/4 teaspoon nutmeg

BAKED SEA BASS A LA VERACRUZ

Sprinkle fish with lime juice, salt, and pepper and arrange in an 11×14×2-inch baking pan. In a large skillet, heat oil over moderate heat. Add onion and sauté 5 minutes, or until soft. Add garlic; sauté 1 minute. Drain tomatoes, reserving juice, and add to skillet, breaking up tomatoes with a spoon. Add remaining ingredients. Bring to a boil, reduce heat to moderate and simmer, uncovered, 15 minutes. If necessary, add some of the reserved tomato juice to the sauce during cooking. Pour sauce over fish and bake, uncovered, in convection oven on rack position 2 at 350° for 35 minutes. Serve with rice and a tart cabbage salad.

6 to 8 servings

1 5-pound sea bass or red snapper, cleaned, gills and head removed; or 3 pounds thick fillets of any white-fleshed fish
Juice of 1 lime or lemon
Salt and pepper
1/4 cup olive oil
2 cups diced onion
2 tablespoons chopped garlic
1 can (35 ounces) whole peeled tomatoes
1 cup small pimiento-stuffed olives
1 can (4 ounces) chopped hot green chilies, drained
1/4 cup drained capers
1 teaspoon oregano
1 teaspoon salt
1/4 teaspoon hot pepper sauce

Baked Sea Bass à la Veracruz

LOBSTER THERMIDOR

4 lobsters (1 1/2 to
   2 pounds each)
1/4 cup butter
1 pound mushrooms,
   thinly sliced
3 tablespoons finely
   minced shallots
   Salt and pepper
1 tablespoon chopped
   pimiento
2 tablespoons finely
   chopped parsley,
   divided
3/4 cup soft bread crumbs
2 teaspoons
   Worcestershire sauce
3 tablespoons brandy
1/2 cup dry sherry
1 cup heavy cream
3 egg yolks, lightly beaten
2 drops hot pepper sauce
3/4 cup grated Parmesan cheese
   Paprika

Place lobsters in boiling water and cook 10 to 12 minutes. Drain under cold water. Remove claws, crack, and remove meat. Cut lobsters in half lengthwise, remove meat, and discard roe (or eat it yourself!). Reserve shells. Cut lobster meat into small chunks. Melt butter in medium-size saucepan and sauté mushrooms and shallots 2 to 3 minutes. Add lobster meat, salt, pepper, pimiento, 1 tablespoon parsley, bread crumbs, and Worcestershire and stir. Add brandy and sherry, remove from heat and stir. Combine cream and egg yolks in a small bowl. Slowly add a few teaspoons of hot liquid from saucepan and mix well. Pour back into saucepan and return to very low heat. Stir until thickened. Do not boil. Add 1 or 2 drops of hot pepper sauce. Spoon mixture into reserved shells, dividing equally. Place in a 10×15×1-inch baking pan. Sprinkle with cheese and paprika. Bake in convection oven on rack position 2 at 350° for 20 minutes. Garnish with remaining chopped parsley and serve immediately.

4 servings

CRAB CASSEROLE

2 packages (6 ounces
   each) frozen crab
   meat, thawed
   and drained
1 can (10 1/2 ounces)
   cream of shrimp
   soup, undiluted
1 clove garlic, crushed
2/3 cup milk
1 cup mayonnaise
2 cups fine spaghetti,
   broken into 3-inch
   pieces
1/2 cup grated Cheddar
   cheese

Mix the crab meat, soup, garlic, milk, mayonnaise, and spaghetti in a shallow 7×11-inch casserole. Sprinkle with cheese. Bake in convection oven on rack position 2 at 350° for 35 to 40 minutes. Stir every 15 minutes, or until cheese is melted. Serve hot.

Note: This casserole with hot rolls and a green salad makes an elegant luncheon. Smaller servings are delicious and unusual as a first course.

6 servings

Lobster Thermidor

CREOLE FILLETS

1 pound fillets of sole
   or flounder
Salt and pepper
Juice of 1 lemon
2 cups Louisiana Creole
   Sauce (page 89)

Wash fillets and pat dry. Place in an oven-proof 9×13×2-inch baking dish in 1 layer. Season both sides with salt, pepper, and lemon juice. Spoon Creole Sauce over fish and bake in convection oven on rack position 2 in 300° oven for 15 minutes, or until fish flakes easily with a fork.

4 servings

BAKED FISH FILLETS WITH ARTICHOKES

1 pound fillets of sole
   or flounder, fresh
   or frozen
1/4 teaspoon salt
1/4 teaspoon pepper
1 1/2 cups peeled, seeded,
   and diced tomatoes
1 jar (6 ounces)
   marinated
   artichokes, sliced
1/2 cup chopped mushrooms
1/2 cup dry white wine
1 tablespoon butter
   or margarine
1/4 cup snipped parsley
   or 1 tablespoon
   dry parsley

If fish is frozen, thaw enough to separate fillets. Lay fish flat in a single layer in a 9×13-inch baking dish. Sprinkle with salt and pepper. Top fish with tomatoes, artichokes, mushrooms, and wine; dot with butter. Bake in convection oven on rack position 2 at 400° for 15 minutes, or until fish and vegetables are tender. Sprinkle with parsley.

4 servings

PASTA

SPINACH AND MUSHROOM LASAGNA

Cook lasagna in rapidly boiling salted water 5 to 7 minutes. Drain in a colander and rinse with cold water. Carefully hang each strip over edge of the colander to prevent sticking. Melt 6 tablespoons of butter in a large saucepan over moderate heat. Add onion and sauté 5 minutes, stirring often, until transparent. Sprinkle with flour and cook 1 minute, stirring constantly. Stir in the broth, cream, and wine and bring to a boil. Reduce heat and simmer 5 minutes, stirring often, or until sauce is thickened and smooth. Stir in salt, pepper, and nutmeg. Melt the remaining 2 tablespoons butter in medium-size skillet and sauté mushrooms about 3 minutes. Sprinkle with salt and pepper and set aside. Butter an 11×15×2-inch baking dish. Spread about 1 cup of sauce in bottom of dish. Arrange a third of the noodles in a single layer over sauce. Spoon spinach over noodles and sprinkle with 1 cup Swiss cheese. Top with half the remaining pasta and spoon over the mushrooms. Sprinkle with the remaining 1 cup Swiss cheese and another cup of sauce. Arrange remaining noodles on top, pour over the remaining sauce and sprinkle with Parmesan cheese. Bake in convection oven on rack position 2 at 375° for 30 minutes, or until lasagna is golden brown and bubbling. Let stand at least 10 minutes before cutting into squares to serve.

Another way: 3 cups of homemade or frozen, thawed, creamed spinach may be substituted for the frozen spinach soufflé. The lasagna can be assembled ahead of time, covered and refrigerated. To reheat, bake in convection oven on rack position 2 at 350° for 45 to 60 minutes, or until golden brown and heated through.

8 servings

1 package (16 ounces) lasagna
8 tablespoons butter or margarine, divided
1 cup chopped onion
6 tablespoons all-purpose flour
2 1/2 cups chicken broth
1 cup heavy cream
1/2 cup dry white wine or dry vermouth
1/2 teaspoon salt
1/4 teaspoon pepper
1/4 teaspoon nutmeg
1 pound fresh mushrooms, sliced
3 packages (10 ounces each) frozen spinach soufflé, thawed
2 cups grated Swiss cheese, divided
1/2 cup grated Parmesan cheese

MANICOTTI

Combine the ricotta, mozzarella, and 1/3 cup Parmesan cheese with eggs, parsley, and salt in small bowl; set aside. Cook manicotti shells according to package directions. Drain and fill with cheese mixture. Place small amount spaghetti sauce in bottom of 13×9-inch pan. Arrange stuffed shells on sauce. Top with additional sauce and remaining 1/3 cup Parmesan cheese. Cover and bake in convection oven in center of the rack in position 1 at 350° for 25 minutes. Uncover and bake an additional 15 minutes. Let stand 5 minutes and serve.

6 servings

4 cups ricotta cheese
8 ounces mozzarella cheese, cut in small cubes
2/3 cup grated Parmesan cheese, divided
2 eggs
2 tablespoons chopped parsley or 2 teaspoons dry parsley
1 teaspoon salt
16 ounces manicotti shells
Oven Spaghetti Sauce

Oven Spaghetti Sauce

Turn on convection oven to 375°. Combine olive oil, garlic, and onion in 3-quart casserole. Place on rack position 2 and bake 10 minutes. Dissolve bouillon cube in 1 cup boiling water. Crush tomatoes and stir with tomato paste, bouillon, basil, parsley, sugar, and salt into onion mixture. Return to oven and cook, covered, 15 minutes, or until boiling. Remove cover and cook an additional 45 to 60 minutes, or until thick. Use with Manicotti or other pasta dishes.

Note: This sauce freezes well. Make two batches and freeze one to use later. Reheat frozen sauce in a double boiler to prevent scorching.

6 servings

3 tablespoons olive oil
1 clove garlic, minced
1/4 cup chopped onion
1 beef bouillon cube
1 cup boiling water
1 can (28 ounces) tomatoes
1 can (6 ounces) tomato paste
3 leaves basil, chopped, or 1 teaspoon dried basil
2 tablespoons chopped parsley or 2 teaspoons dry parsley
1/2 teaspoon sugar
1/2 teaspoon salt

Manicotti

MILAN LASAGNA

1/2 pound ground beef
1/2 pound hot Italian
    sausage
1/2 teaspoon salt
1/4 teaspoon pepper
1/2 teaspoon oregano
1/2 cup chopped onion
  1 can (29 ounces)
    tomato sauce
  1 can (12 ounces)
    tomato paste
  1 can (8 ounces)
    sliced mushrooms
    with liquid
  1 bay leaf
  1 package (16 ounces)
    lasagna
  2 cups ricotta cheese
16 ounces sliced
    mozzarella cheese

Brown ground beef and sausage in saucepan over medium heat and drain. Add salt, pepper, oregano, and onion. Stir in tomato sauce, tomato paste, mushrooms, and bay leaf. Simmer, covered, over low heat for 1 hour. Discard bay leaf.

Cook lasagna according to package directions. Grease an 11×14×2-inch pan. Beginning with lasagna, layer sauce, ricotta, and mozzarella in pan. Continue layering until all the lasagna and cheese are used. Save some sauce to spread over last layer of lasagna. Bake in convection oven on position 2 at 300° about 30 minutes, until hot and bubbly.

Lasagna may be assembled ahead of time and refrigerated, tightly covered. When ready to serve, bake at 300° for 1 hour.

8 servings

LASAGNA ROLLS

   1 package (12 ounces)
    lasagna, cooked
    and cooled
   1 cup ricotta cheese
1 1/2 cups grated Parmesan
    cheese
  1/4 cup minced parsley or
    1 tablespoon dry
    parsley
  1/4 cup minced onion
   1 egg yolk
  1/2 teaspoon garlic
    powder or 1 small
    clove garlic,
    minced
  1/2 teaspoon salt
  1/4 teaspoon oregano
  1/4 teaspoon pepper
   1 can (15 ounces)
    herbed tomato sauce

Cook lasagna according to package directions; drain and set aside.

Combine thoroughly all ingredients except lasagna and tomato sauce. Spread cheese mixture on each lasagna and roll up. Stand vertically in a greased 8-inch square pan. Pour tomato sauce over pasta. Bake in convection oven on rack position 2 at 350° for 25 minutes. Serve hot with garlic bread and green salad.

Note: You may prepare Lasagna Rolls in advance to the point the tomato sauce is added. Cover tightly and store in refrigerator or freezer for later use.

6 servings

VEGETABLES

COOKING FROZEN VEGETABLES IN THE CONVECTION OVEN

While your convection oven is heated to cook main courses, it is easy and economical to cook frozen vegetables simultaneously. Most popular vegetables are delicious cooked by the following method:

Place frozen vegetables, still in a hard block, on a couple of thicknesses of aluminum foil or in a small baking dish with a tight-fitting lid. Sprinkle with 1/4 teaspoon salt and top with 2 tablespoons butter or margarine. Seal foil or cover tightly; place in convection oven on rack position 2 or 3 at 325°. (If your main dish is cooking at another temperature, adjust the following times slightly.)

Vegetable (10-ounce package)	Cooking time at 325° in Convection Oven
French-cut green beans	50 minutes
Broccoli spears	45 minutes
Peas	40 minutes
Cut whole-kernel corn	40 minutes
Cauliflower	55 minutes
Leaf spinach	60 minutes
Lima beans	65 minutes
Asparagus spears	60 minutes
Snow peas (6-ounce package)	45 minutes

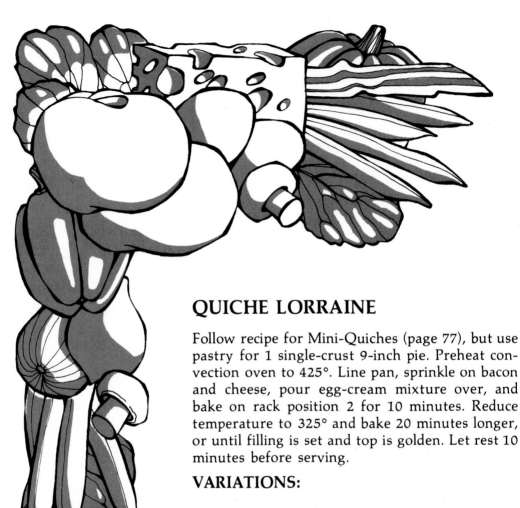

QUICHE LORRAINE

Follow recipe for Mini-Quiches (page 77), but use pastry for 1 single-crust 9-inch pie. Preheat convection oven to 425°. Line pan, sprinkle on bacon and cheese, pour egg-cream mixture over, and bake on rack position 2 for 10 minutes. Reduce temperature to 325° and bake 20 minutes longer, or until filling is set and top is golden. Let rest 10 minutes before serving.

VARIATIONS:

Spinach Quiche

Follow recipe for Quiche Lorraine, but eliminate bacon and substitute 1/4 cup grated Parmesan cheese for Swiss cheese. Add 1 package (10 ounces) frozen chopped spinach, thawed and very well drained, to custard mixture.

Vegetable Quiche

Follow recipe for Quiche Lorraine, but instead of Swiss cheese, use 1/2 cup shredded Cheddar cheese and 1 cup lightly cooked chopped green vegetables, well drained. Asparagus, fresh, frozen, or canned; broccoli; green beans; summer squash; fresh tomatoes, peeled, seeded, and chopped; artichoke hearts — all are good. Add 1/2 teaspoon dry mustard to custard mixture.

CHEESE SOUFFLE

Remove top rack of oven. Generously butter a 1 1/2-quart soufflé dish. Butter one side of a long piece of aluminum foil and make a collar, with buttered side facing in. Melt butter in saucepan; add flour and stir to make a roux. Gradually add milk and stir until thickened. Remove from heat. Slowly add a small amount of sauce base to beaten egg yolks, stirring vigorously. Pour egg mixture back into saucepan slowly, beating constantly. Stir in cheese, mustard, and cayenne. Transfer to large bowl. Preheat convection oven to 400°. Beat egg whites and salt in separate bowl until foamy. Add cream of tartar and beat until stiff peaks form. Gently fold egg whites into cheese mixture. Fill prepared dish. Place in center of oven on rack position 2. Reduce oven temperature to 375°. Bake 25 to 30 minutes. Remove collar; serve immediately.

4 servings

Nice to know: An elegant and easy oven meal features Cheese Soufflé, Asparagus Spears (page 123), and French Bread (page 147).

2 1/2 tablespoons butter
3 tablespoons
all-purpose flour
1 cup milk
4 egg yolks,
lightly beaten
3/4 cup grated cheese,
a combination of
Swiss and Parmesan
1/2 teaspoon prepared
mustard
Dash cayenne
5 egg whites, at room
temperature
Pinch salt
1/8 teaspoon cream
of tartar

GREEN BEAN AND EGG CASSEROLE

Cook the green beans and drain. Melt butter in saucepan and sauté onion until transparent; remove from heat; stir in flour until thick paste forms, then gradually stir in milk. Cook, stirring constantly, until sauce is smooth and thick. Add salt, pepper, Worcestershire, and parsley. Butter 1-quart casserole and fill with alternate layers of beans, egg, sauce. Combine crumbs and cheese; sprinkle over top of casserole. Bake in convection oven on rack position 2 at 325° for 15 to 20 minutes, or until hot and browned.

4 servings

1 package (9 ounces)
frozen green beans
1/4 cup butter
or margarine
1/4 cup minced onion
1/4 cup all-purpose flour
2 cups milk, warmed
1 teaspoon salt
Dash pepper
1/4 teaspoon
Worcestershire sauce
2 tablespoons minced
parsley
4 hard-cooked eggs,
sliced
1/4 cup dry bread crumbs
1/2 cup grated Parmesan
cheese

MUSHROOM-HERB STUFFED TOMATOES

6 medium-size tomatoes
2 tablespoons chopped basil
3 tablespoons butter or margarine
2 cloves garlic, minced
1 small onion, finely chopped
1 pound mushrooms, freshly chopped
1 teaspoon oregano
3 tablespoons finely chopped parsley
1/4 cup seasoned dry bread crumbs
Salt and freshly ground pepper
4 tablespoons grated Parmesan cheese, divided

Remove stems from tomatoes and gently squeeze out juice and seeds. Hollow out and lightly salt the inside of tomatoes. Add a pinch of basil to each. Melt butter in skillet and sauté garlic and onion until transparent. Add mushrooms (from which as much liquid as possible has been squeezed) and cook until all the moisture has evaporated. Add oregano, parsley, bread crumbs, salt, pepper, and 2 tablespoons cheese. Stir to combine. Lightly grease an 8-inch round cake dish. Stuff each tomato with mushroom mixture and sprinkle tops with remaining 2 tablespoons of cheese. Bake in convection oven on rack position 2 at 350° for 20 minutes. Tomatoes should be fork tender but firm. Serve with broiled fish and meat.

Note: The fresh basil, parsley, and freshly ground pepper are important in this recipe. Make it when fresh herbs are available in abundance.

6 servings

Nice to know: Chop mushrooms in food processor. Place in linen dish towel and twist to squeeze out liquid. Save tomato juice and pulp for soup, stews, and chili dishes.

BROCCOLI AND CHEESE TIMBALE

2 packages (10 ounces each) frozen chopped broccoli, thawed and thoroughly drained
6 eggs
1/4 cup minced onion
1 cup fresh bread crumbs
3/4 cup grated Swiss cheese
1/4 cup chopped parsley
1/2 cup heavy cream
1 teaspoon salt
1/4 teaspoon nutmeg
1/8 teaspoon cayenne

Combine all ingredients in a large bowl and blend well. Turn into a buttered 2-quart casserole. Place casserole in larger shallow pan and fill pan with boiling water to a depth of 2 inches. Place in convection oven on rack position 2 and bake at 350° for 30 minutes. Reduce oven temperature to 325° and bake 30 minutes longer. Remove timbale from oven and from larger pan and let stand 10 minutes before unmolding. Serve cut in wedges.

8 servings

Provençale Rice and Vegetable Gratin (page 128)
Broccoli and Cheese Timbale
Mushroom-Herb Stuffed Tomatoes

OVEN RATATOUILLE

1 small eggplant
3 medium-size zucchini
1/2 cup olive oil
2 large onions, sliced
6 large cloves garlic,
   minced
2 green peppers, cored,
   seeded, and sliced
3 large ripe tomatoes,
   cut in chunks
2 teaspoons salt
1/4 teaspoon pepper
2 tablespoons chopped
   basil
1/2 cup chopped parsley

Remove and discard stem end of eggplant and cut eggplant into 1-inch cubes. Cut zucchini into slices 1/4-inch thick. Place eggplant and zucchini in the bottom of a large shallow baking pan and set aside. Heat oil in a large skillet over moderate heat. Add onions, garlic, peppers, and tomatoes and sauté 5 minutes, stirring often. Spoon onion mixture over eggplant and zucchini and sprinkle with the salt, pepper, basil, and parsley. Place in convection oven on rack position 2 and bake at 400° for 30 minutes, or until vegetables are tender but still hold their shape. Although ratatouille can be served immediately, it is better if it is made a day or two in advance. Serve hot or cold.

8 servings

PROVENÇALE RICE AND VEGETABLE GRATIN

1/4 cup olive oil
1 cup chopped onion
2 pounds zucchini,
   grated and squeezed
   dry or 2 packages
   (10 ounces each)
   frozen chopped
   spinach, thawed and
   thoroughly drained
2 large cloves garlic,
   minced
2 green or red peppers,
   cored, seeded, and
   thinly sliced
2 tablespoons
   all-purpose flour
2 cups milk
2 cups cooked rice
1 teaspoon salt
1 teaspoon pepper
3/4 cup grated Parmesan
   cheese, divided

Heat oil in a large skillet over moderate heat. Add onion and zucchini or spinach and sauté 3 minutes. Add garlic and peppers and sauté 3 minutes longer. Sprinkle with flour and cook 1 minute. Add milk and bring to a boil, stirring frequently until liquid begins to thicken. Simmer 2 minutes. Remove from heat and stir in rice, salt, pepper, and 1/4 cup of the cheese. Pour mixture into an 11-inch-long gratin dish and sprinkle with the remaining 1/2 cup cheese. Bake in convection oven on rack position 3 at 400° for 20 to 25 minutes, or until top is golden and rice has absorbed most of the liquid. Serve directly from dish.

6 servings

Nice to know: Provençale Rice is a delicious side dish, but it is also a good light main course. Serve with a fruit dessert for contrast.

BROCCOLI-ONION CASSEROLE

Cook broccoli according to package directions; drain. Cook onions in boiling salted water until tender; drain. In a 2-quart saucepan melt 2 tablespoons butter; blend in flour, salt, and pepper. Add milk. Cook on medium heat and stir until thick. Reduce heat and stir in cream cheese until smooth. Stir in vegetables. Pour into 2-quart casserole. Melt remaining butter and toss with bread crumbs and cheese. Sprinkle over casserole and bake in convection oven on rack position 3 at 350° for 15 minutes.

10 servings

2 packages (10 ounces each) frozen chopped broccoli
2 cups frozen small whole onions
4 tablespoons butter or margarine, divided
2 tablespoons all-purpose flour
1/4 teaspoon salt
1/8 teaspoon white pepper
1 cup milk, warmed
1 package (3 ounces) cream cheese, cut up
1 cup dry bread crumbs
1/4 cup grated Parmesan cheese

CREAMY CAULIFLOWERETS

Clean cauliflower; cut into flowerets and cook in salted boiling water until barely tender. Blend crumbs, flour, and cheese. Put half this mixture into well-buttered 9-inch pie pan. Arrange drained cauliflower evenly in pie pan. Beat sour cream, eggs, salt, and pepper; pour over cauliflower. Sprinkle remaining crumb mixture evenly over top. Bake in convection oven on rack position 2 at 350° for 20 to 25 minutes, or until heated through and browned.

6 servings

1 medium-size cauliflower
1/2 cup dry bread crumbs
2 tablespoons all-purpose flour
1/2 cup grated Cheddar or Parmesan cheese
1 cup dairy sour cream
2 eggs
1/2 teaspoon salt
1/8 teaspoon white pepper

STUFFED ACORN SQUASH

4 small acorn squash
4 tablespoons chopped
   onion
1 cup finely diced
   Muenster cheese
3/4 cup heavy cream
   Salt and pepper

Cut a 1-inch thick "cap" from the top of each squash. Reserve caps, scoop seeds out and discard. Place 1 tablespoon of onion, 1/4 cup of cheese, and 3 tablespoons of cream in the cavity of each squash. Sprinkle lightly with salt and pepper. Cover squash with the caps and place in a shallow baking pan just large enough to hold them. Bake in convection oven on rack position 2 at 350° for 45 minutes. Remove caps from squash and increase oven temperature to 450°. Bake 10 to 15 minutes longer, or until filling puffs up and browns.

4 servings

OLD-FASHIONED EGGPLANT CASSEROLE

2 large eggplants
   (about 1 1/2 to
   2 pounds each)
1/2 cup butter
   or margarine
1 cup chopped onion
1 green pepper, cored,
   seeded, and chopped
4 eggs, separated
1/2 cup cracker crumbs
1/2 cup chopped parsley
2 cups grated sharp
   Cheddar cheese
1 teaspoon salt
1/4 teaspoon pepper
1/2 teaspoon thyme

Remove and discard stem ends of eggplants. Peel and quarter eggplants lengthwise. Place in large pot of boiling salted water; cover. When water returns to boil, reduce heat and simmer 7 to 10 minutes, or until eggplant is just tender. Drain. Melt butter in a large skillet. Add onion and green pepper and sauté 5 minutes, stirring often, until onion is transparent. Add eggplant to skillet and cook about 1 minute, mashing eggplant with the side of a spoon to a fairly smooth purée. Beat egg yolks and stir into eggplant with crumbs, parsley, cheese, salt, pepper, and thyme. Beat egg whites until stiff and fold in. Turn mixture into a buttered 2-quart casserole and bake in convection oven on rack position 2 at 350° for 45 minutes, or until puffed and lightly browned. Serve immediately with tomato sauce or stewed tomatoes and hot corn muffins.

Note: This recipe may be made with almost any vegetable: summer squash, zucchini, green beans, broccoli, winter squash, or cauliflower.

8 servings

Stuffed Acorn Squash

STUFFED EGGPLANT

3 medium-size eggplants
3 tablespoons butter
   or margarine
1 large onion, chopped
3 cloves garlic, minced
1/3 cup finely chopped
   parsley
1 1/2 pounds extra lean
   ground beef
1/2 cup seasoned dry
   bread crumbs
3 eggs, lightly beaten
3/4 cup grated Parmesan
   cheese
1 cup shredded
   mozzarella cheese
Salt and pepper
6 slices mozzarella
   cheese
Paprika
Parsley sprigs

Wash and trim ends of eggplant and cut in half lengthwise. Place in boiling salted water for 5 to 8 minutes. Drain in colander and set on paper towels to cool. Meanwhile, melt butter in medium-size skillet and sauté onion and garlic until transparent. Add parsely and remove from heat. Place meat in large mixing bowl; add onion mixture. Hollow out eggplants leaving 1/2 inch pulp in eggplant shell. Reserve shells. Discard seeds, reserving scooped-out pulp. Cut pulp into small chunks and add to meat. Add bread crumbs, eggs, Parmesan , shredded mozzarella, salt, and pepper. Stir with large wooden spoon. Spoon into reserved shells. Place in lightly greased shallow baking dish, large enough to hold all filled halves in one layer, about 11×14×2 inches. Bake eggplant in convection oven on rack position 2 at 325° for 20 minutes. Remove from oven; place 1 slice of mozzarella on top of each filled eggplant. Sprinkle with paprika and return to oven. Continue cooking 8 to 10 minutes longer, or until cheese is golden brown. Remove from dish with slotted spoon and serve on platter garnished with sprigs of parsley.

Serve with a tossed green salad and hot rolls for a very filling, complete meal.

6 servings

SWEET POTATO SOUFFLE

3 cups mashed sweet
   potatoes
6 eggs, separated
1/2 cup light cream
1/2 teaspoon salt
1 cup milk
1/2 cup butter or
   margarine, melted
1 teaspoon lemon juice

Grease a 2 1/2- to 3-quart soufflé dish or casserole. Beat sweet potatoes and egg yolks together in a large bowl. Add all other ingredients except egg whites and mix well. Beat egg whites until very stiff and fold into potato mixture. Pour into prepared dish and bake in convection oven on rack position 2 at 375° for 45 minutes, or until a knife inserted in center comes out clean. Serve at once.

8 to 10 servings

SCALLOPED GARLIC POTATOES

Place potatoes in a buttered 2-quart casserole. In a small saucepan, bring cream to a boil with garlic, salt, and pepper, and pour over potatoes. Dot with butter and sprinkle with paprika. Bake in convection oven on rack position 2 at 400° for 35 to 45 minutes, or until top is golden and crisp and potatoes are tender when pierced with a knife.

8 to 10 servings

6 to 8 large all-purpose potatoes, thinly sliced
2 cups light cream
2 large cloves garlic, minced
2 teaspoons salt
1/4 teaspoon white pepper
6 tablespoons butter
Paprika

CRISP PAN POTATOES

Arrange potatoes in a buttered 9×11×2-inch oven-to-table baking dish. Sprinkle with salt and pepper and drizzle with butter. Bake in convection oven on rack position 2 at 400° for 30 minutes, or until top of potatoes is crisp and golden brown. Garnish with paprika and sprigs of parsley. Serve directly from dish.

6 servings

6 large baking potatoes, cut into 1/8-inch thick slices
Salt and pepper
1/2 cup butter or margarine, melted
Paprika
Parsley sprigs

BOURBON SWEET POTATOES

Drain yams. In large electric mixer bowl, combine all ingredients except marshmallows and nuts; beat until fluffy, or purée yams in food processor and then mix with other ingredients. Place in 2-quart casserole. Bake in convection oven on rack position 2 at 325° for 40 minutes. Remove from oven; place marshmallows in decorative fashion; sprinkle with walnuts. Return to oven for 2 minutes, or until marshmallows are slightly melted and golden in color. Serve hot.

6 to 8 servings

2 cans (40 ounces) yams
1/2 cup bourbon
1/2 cup liquid brown sugar or 1 cup firmly packed brown sugar
1/3 cup orange juice
1/4 cup butter or margarine
1/2 teaspoon salt
1/2 teaspoon nutmeg
1/2 teaspoon cinnamon
1/2 teaspoon clove
10 to 12 marshmallows
1/2 cup chopped walnuts

MUSHROOM-RICE PILAF

4   tablespoons butter
1   onion, sliced
1/2   pound mushrooms, sliced
1   can (10 3/4 ounces)
      condensed chicken
      broth, undiluted
1   cup long-grained rice
1/2   teaspoon salt
      Freshly ground pepper

In large skillet, melt butter; sauté onion until softened but not browned. Add mushrooms and sauté 5 minutes longer. Place chicken broth, rice, salt, and pepper in a 1-quart casserole. Add onion and mushrooms and stir to combine. Cover and bake in convection oven on rack position 2 at 325° for 40 to 45 minutes, or until all liquid is absorbed. Serve hot.

4 servings

ELEGANT CORN CASSEROLE

Beat egg yolks; mix in corn, flour, sugar, salt, and pepper. Beat egg whites until stiff. Fold into corn mixture. Grease a 1-quart straight-sided baking dish. Pile corn mixture lightly in dish. Bake in convection oven on rack position 2 at 350° for 35 minutes, or until a knife inserted in center comes out clean. Serve at once. This soufflé-like dish will look its best just out of the oven.

6 servings

2 eggs, separated
1 can (16 ounces) white cream-style corn
2 tablespoons all-purpose flour
1 teaspoon sugar
1 teaspoon salt
1/4 teaspoon white pepper

BASIC BOSTON BAKED BEANS

Place beans in a large pot with water to cover and soak overnight. Drain beans and place in a large heavy casserole with the remaining ingredients; add boiling water to cover. Cover and bake in convection oven on rack position 2 at 250° for 5 hours, or until beans are very tender and sauce is glazed and thickened. Remove cover during final 10 minutes of cooking.

12 servings

2 pounds dried pea beans
1 cup diced onion
3/4 cup catsup
1/2 cup firmly packed dark brown sugar
1/4 cup molasses
1/4 teaspoon dry mustard
4 teaspoons salt
1/2 pound salt pork, diced (about 1 cup)

SPANISH LIMA BEANS

Brown bacon and onion in skillet. Add flour, seasonings, and tomatoes. Add beans, stir, and pour into buttered 1 1/2-quart casserole. Sprinkle with crumbs and dot with butter. Bake, uncovered, in convection oven on rack position 2 at 350° for 25 to 30 minutes.

6 to 8 servings

4 slices bacon, diced
1/2 cup chopped onion
2 tablespoons all-purpose flour
1 bay leaf
Salt
Pepper
Paprika
2 cups cooked tomatoes
2 cups cooked fresh lima beans or 10 ounces frozen lima beans
1/2 cup dry bread crumbs
2 tablespoons butter

BAKED WILD RICE CASSEROLE

1 cup wild rice
1 cup grated Cheddar
     cheese, divided
1 can (8 1/4 ounces)
     stewed tomatoes
8 ounces mushrooms,
     sliced
1 cup boiling water
1/2 cup chopped onion
1/4 cup vegetable oil
1 teaspoon salt
1/4 teaspoon pepper
1/3 cup chopped
     ripe olives

Wash rice; cover with 1 quart hot water and let stand 6 hours or overnight. Drain rice and combine with all other ingredients except 1/4 cup cheese in a 2-quart casserole. Cover and bake in convection oven on rack position 2 at 350° for 1 hour, stirring once; the rice should be tender and fluffed. Uncover and sprinkle with 1/4 cup cheese; return to oven for 5 minutes to melt cheese. If casserole seems dry during cooking, add water or chicken stock; if moist, bake a few minutes longer.

6 to 8 servings

WINTER SQUASH AND APPLE PUREE

1 large butternut
     squash
3 medium-size apples,
     such as McIntosh,
     Rome Beauty,
     or Pippin
3/4 cup apple juice or
     cider
6 tablespoons butter or
     margarine, divided
1 teaspoon salt
1/4 teaspoon pepper
1/2 cup finely chopped
     pecans
1/2 cup fine dry
     bread crumbs

Remove and discard stem end of squash. Cut squash in half lengthwise, scoop out seeds and discard. Peel, core, and cut apples in half. Arrange squash, cut side down, in a large shallow baking pan. Surround with apples and pour apple juice over. Bake in convection oven on rack position 2 at 350° for 50 to 60 minutes, or until squash is very tender when pierced with a fork. When squash is cool enough to handle, scrape pulp from skin and purée with apples in food processor, blender, or with food mill. It will be necessary to purée mixture in 2 batches. Transfer purée to a bowl and stir in 4 tablespoons of butter, salt, and pepper. Grease a 1-quart casserole and pour in purée. Combine the nuts and bread crumbs, and sprinkle over purée. Dot with the remaining 2 tablespoons of butter. Bake in convection oven on rack position 3 at 375° for 20 minutes, or until crumbs are lightly browned and crisp.

8 servings

Nice to know: Dish can be prepared ahead of time up to the final baking. Cover and refrigerate. To reheat, place on rack position 3 and bake at 350° for 40 minutes, or until purée is heated through and crumbs are crisp and golden.

ZUCCHINI PARMESAN

Heat oil in a large skillet over moderate heat. Add sausage and sauté 10 minutes, breaking up sausage with the side of a spoon. Add onion and garlic and cook until the onion is transparent. Reserve 2 tablespoons sausage mixture for ricotta filling. Add tomato sauce, oregano, basil, salt, and pepper to skillet and simmer 5 minutes. Place ricotta in small bowl, add reserved 2 tablespoons sausage mixture, egg, parsley, salt, and pepper. Remove ends of zucchini and discard. Slice the zucchini lengthwise into slices 1/4 inch thick. Spread a little of the meat sauce in the bottom of a 9×11×2-inch baking dish and arrange zucchini in a single layer over sauce. Spread with ricotta mixture and sprinkle with 1/4 cup of the Parmesan cheese. Pour remaining meat sauce over. Arrange mozzarella slices on top and sprinkle with the remaining 3/4 cup Parmesan cheese. Bake in convection oven on rack position 2 at 375° for 30 minutes, or until heated through and cheese is golden and bubbling. Let stand 10 minutes before cutting into squares.

Note: When a great deal of grated Parmesan cheese is called for in a recipe, it is both delicious and economical to buy the cheese in bulk and grate it yourself. A blender or food processor does the job fast; a hand grater works fine. Parmesan keeps well. Cover with plastic wrap and refrigerate.

8 servings

1 tablespoon olive oil
1 pound mild (sweet) Italian sausage, casing removed
2 cups chopped onion
4 large cloves garlic, minced
1 can (15 ounces) tomato sauce
1 teaspoon oregano
1 teaspoon basil
Salt and pepper
2 cups ricotta cheese
1 egg, lightly beaten
1/4 cup chopped parsley or 1 tablespoon dry parsley
1/4 teaspoon salt
1/4 teaspoon pepper
4 large zucchini (about 2 1/2 pounds)
1 cup grated Parmesan cheese, divided
8 ounces mozzarella cheese, thinly sliced

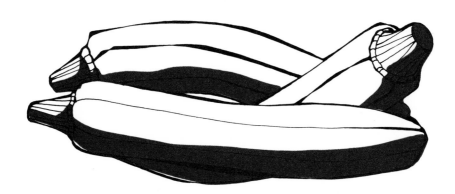

CHEDDAR AND TOMATO CASSEROLE

2 tablespoons butter
   or margarine
1 cup chopped onion
1 can (28 ounces) whole
   tomatoes, drained
1 1/2 cups grated sharp
   Cheddar cheese,
   divided
1 cup crushed saltines
4 eggs
1/2 teaspoon salt
1/4 teaspoon pepper
1/2 teaspoon basil
   or thyme

Melt butter in a medium-size skillet over moderate heat. Add onion and sauté 3 minutes, stirring often. Stir in tomatoes, breaking them up with a spoon, and cook about 5 minutes longer, or until most of the liquid has evaporated. Remove pan from heat and stir in 1 cup Cheddar cheese and remaining ingredients. Butter a 1-quart casserole and pour in tomato mixture. Sprinkle with the reserved 1/2 cup cheese. Bake in convection oven on rack position 2 at 350° for 30 minutes, or until pudding is puffed and top is lightly browned. Let stand 5 minutes before serving.

4 to 6 servings

BEEF BURGUNDY SOUP

1 large onion, sliced
1 cup sliced mushrooms
2 pounds sirloin steak
   cut in 1-inch cubes
1/2 teaspoon salt
1/4 teaspoon marjoram
1/4 teaspoon pepper
2 cups rich beef stock
   or bouillon
1 1/4 cups Burgundy wine

Place onion, mushrooms, and steak in a greased 9×13-inch pan. Mix 1 cup water with all other ingredients except the Burgundy and pour over steak and vegetables. Bake in convection oven on rack position 2 at 375° for 1 hour and 30 minutes. Stir after 1 hour in oven. Add Burgundy; stir and bake an additional 15 minutes. Serve hot with warm hard rolls.

6 servings

ICED CUCUMBER SOUP

4 cups chicken stock
3 medium-size potatoes,
   thinly sliced
1 small onion, chopped
3 medium-size cucumbers,
   seeded, peeled,
   and diced
1 tablespoon chopped
   chives or 1 teaspoon
   dry chives
16 ounces dairy
   sour cream

Combine all ingredients except sour cream in a 9×13-inch baking pan. Bake in convection oven on rack position 2 at 350° for 1 hour. Chill in refrigerator 2 hours and add sour cream. Mix well. Chill an additional 4 hours before serving.

Note: Put the chilled soup in the blender for a smooth soup. Stir in sour cream by hand.

8 servings

OVEN MINESTRONE

Combine all ingredients except macaroni and cheese in an 11×14×3-inch pan. Bake, covered with foil, in convection oven on rack position 2 at 350° for 2 hours. Stir in hot macaroni and sprinkle with cheese. Serve with warm Italian bread to make a hearty meal.

8 to 10 servings

2 carrots, thinly sliced
2 stalks celery, sliced
1 leek, chopped
1 can (30 ounces) kidney beans, drained
1 package (10 ounces) frozen lima beans, thawed
1 cup cubed ham
2 medium-size potatoes, cut in 1/2-inch cubes
1 cup chopped cabbage
1 package (10 ounces) frozen whole-kernel corn, thawed
1 can (15 ounces) tomato sauce with tomato bits
1/2 cup barley
1 teaspoon basil
1/2 teaspoon pepper
1 clove garlic, minced, or 2 teaspoons minced dry garlic
1 tablespoon olive oil
1 teaspoon salt
5 cups beef or chicken stock, or water
1 cup cooked elbow macaroni
1 cup grated Parmesan cheese

HEARTY BEEF-ONION SOUP

1/2 pound ground beef
3 small mild onions,
   thinly sliced
3 teaspoons instant
   beef bouillon
1/4 teaspoon oregano
1/4 teaspoon basil
1/2 teaspoon salt
1/2 teaspoon pepper
4 cups boiling water
4 slices light
   rye bread
4 thin slices
   mozzarella cheese

Brown the ground beef in skillet and drain. Combine beef and all other ingredients except rye bread and cheese in covered 8×11-inch pan. Bake in convection oven on rack position 2 at 375° for 1 hour, or until onion is cooked. Place 1 slice of rye bread in the bottom of each oven-proof soup bowl. Ladle soup over bread and top with a slice of cheese. Return to oven for an additional 10 minutes, or until cheese is melted and slightly brown.

Note: This recipe can easily be doubled. For later use, freeze before bread and cheese are added.

4 servings

CARROT SOUP

1 medium-size onion,
   thinly sliced
6 carrots, sliced
2 medium-size potatoes,
   thinly sliced
2 stalks celery, sliced
1 bay leaf
3 tablespoons chopped
   parsley or
   1 tablespoon dry
   parsley
1/2 teaspoon thyme
1/4 teaspoon pepper
3 1/2 cups rich chicken
   stock or 3 cans
   (10 3/4 ounces each)
   chicken broth

Combine all ingredients with 1 cup water in an 11×14-inch pan. Cover tightly with foil and bake in convection oven on rack position 2 at 350° for 2 hours. Remove and discard bay leaf. Serve hot in warmed bowls.

4 to 6 servings

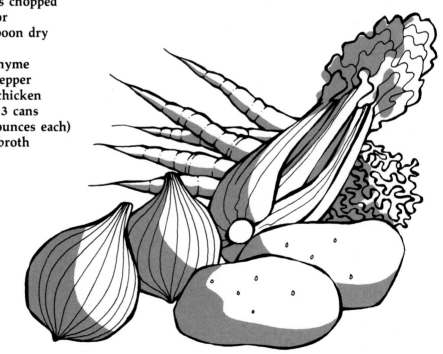

BREAD

COLONIAL SPOON BREAD

In a large bowl combine cornmeal, salt, and sugar; add boiling water and mix. Let stand until lukewarm. Add butter, buttermilk, and baking soda and mix. Beat baking powder with eggs until light and fluffy. Fold eggs and cheese into cornmeal mixture. Pour into a well-greased 1 1/2-quart casserole. Bake in preheated convection oven on rack position 2 at 350° for 45 to 55 minutes. The top should be brown and the center fairly firm. Serve immediately.

8 servings

1 cup yellow cornmeal
1 teaspoon salt
1 teaspoon sugar
1 1/2 cups boiling water
3 tablespoons butter or margarine, melted
1 cup buttermilk
1/2 teaspoon baking soda
1/4 teaspoon baking powder
3 eggs
1/2 cup grated Parmesan cheese, optional

DOUBLE CORN STICKS OR MUFFINS

Generously grease corn stick pan or muffin pan and place in convection oven at 400° to heat. Combine flour, cornmeal, sugar, baking powder, baking soda, and salt in large bowl. Add butter, egg, corn, and buttermilk; mix only enough to moisten ingredients. Pour mixture into heated pan. Place pan on rack position 2. Bake 20 minutes. Serve immediately.

Note: Corn sticks will not brown when cooked in a non-stick pan.

12 corn sticks

1 cup all-purpose flour
1 cup yellow cornmeal
1/3 cup sugar
1 teaspoon baking powder
1/2 teaspoon baking soda
1/2 teaspoon salt
1/4 cup butter or margarine, melted
1 egg
1 can (8 1/2 ounces) cream-style corn
2/3 cup buttermilk

HERB BISCUITS

2 cups all-purpose
   flour
1 tablespoon baking
   powder
1 teaspoon salt
1/3 cup shortening
1 tablespoon chopped
   chives
1 tablespoon chopped
   parsley
3/4 cup milk

Combine flour, baking powder, and salt in large bowl. Cut in shortening with a pastry blender or two knives until mixture resembles coarse meal. Stir in chives and parsley; add milk and quickly blend with fork until mixture leaves sides of bowl. Turn dough onto lightly floured surface and knead 6 to 8 times. Preheat convection oven to 450°. Roll dough 1/2 inch thick; cut with floured 2-inch biscuit cutter. Press dough scraps together and cut again. Place biscuits on ungreased cookie sheet. Bake on rack position 2 for 12 to 15 minutes.

Note: Fresh herbs are important in this recipe. Make Herb Biscuits when they are available.

12 to 16 biscuits

YORKSHIRE PUDDING

2 tablespoons roast
   beef drippings or
   shortening
2 eggs
1 cup milk
1 cup all-purpose flour
1/2 teaspoon salt
   Pinch cayenne

Remove top rack from oven (the pudding will rise very high). Turn convection oven on to 375°. Place drippings in 9-inch glass pie plate and heat in oven, on rack position 2, until very hot and bubbly. Meanwhile, beat eggs slightly. Blend in milk, flour, salt, and cayenne. Pour batter into center of pie plate. Bake 30 to 35 minutes, or until browned. Serve immediately.

Note: If you plan to serve Yorkshire pudding at the same meal as roast beef but have only one oven, heat the pie plate with drippings at 325° the last 10 minutes the meat roasts. When meat is done, remove to let rest before carving. Raise oven temperature to 375° and proceed with recipe.

Yorkshire pudding is traditional with roast beef, but it is also delicious with any meat. It also perks up a meal of leftovers.

4 servings

POPOVERS

Generously grease 8 custard cups or a popover pan with beef drippings or melted shortening. Make batter for Yorkshire Pudding (page 142). Half fill the cups (set custard cups on a baking sheet) and put them in a cold convection oven. Bake at 425° on rack position 2 for 25 minutes. Do not open oven door while popovers bake. When popovers are puffed and lightly browned, turn off heat and cut a small slit in each popover to let steam escape. Let stand 5 minutes in oven to dry out a bit, if desired.

Note: If you wish to make popovers for the same meal as roast beef but have only one oven, heat the greased custard cups or popover pan in the convection oven at 325° the last 10 minutes the meat roasts. Divide drippings or shortening among cups. Make batter for Yorkshire Pudding. When meat is done, remove to let rest before carving. Fill cups half full. Raise temperature to 375°. Bake popovers about 25 minutes, or until lightly browned and puffed.

8 popovers

ZUCCHINI BREAD

Grease and flour two 8×4-inch loaf pans. Combine sugar, oil, eggs, and vanilla in large bowl and mix well. Combine flour, baking soda, ginger, baking powder, salt, and clove in separate bowl and blend into egg mixture. Stir in zucchini, raisins, and nuts. Pour into prepared pans. Bake in center of convection oven on rack position 2 at 325° for 1 hour, or until cake tester inserted in center comes out clean. Cool in pans 20 minutes. Remove from pans and place on wire rack to finish cooling.

2 loaves

1 1/2 cups sugar
2/3 cup vegetable oil
3 eggs
1 teaspoon vanilla extract
2 1/2 cups all-purpose flour
1 teaspoon baking soda
1 teaspoon ginger
1/2 teaspoon baking powder
1 teaspoon salt
1/2 teaspoon clove
2 cups shredded raw zucchini, unpeeled
1/2 cup raisins
1 cup chopped walnuts

BASIC MUFFINS

2 cups sifted
all-purpose flour
3 teaspoons baking
powder
3/4 teaspoon salt
1/3 cup sugar
2 eggs, beaten
1 cup milk
1/4 cup shortening,
melted

Sift together into mixing bowl flour, baking powder, salt, and sugar. Combine eggs, milk, and shortening and add to dry ingredients. Mix quickly, just enough to dampen flour. Fill greased muffin pans two-thirds full. Bake in preheated convection oven on rack position 2 at 350° for 20 to 25 minutes, or until golden brown.

VARIATIONS:

Orange Almond Muffins

To Basic Muffins recipe, add 1/2 cup sugar instead of 1/3 cup, 3/4 cup milk instead of 1 cup, 3 tablespoons fresh orange juice, and 2 tablespoons grated orange rind. Mix as for Basic Muffins. Combine 3 tablespoons ground blanched almonds and 1 tablespoon sugar to sprinkle over top of unbaked batter in muffin pans.

Cinnamon-Raisin Muffins

Add 1 teaspoon cinnamon to dry ingredients in Basic Muffins recipe. Stir in 1/2 cup moist seedless raisins before filling muffin tins.

Blueberry Muffins

Add 1/2 cup sugar instead of 1/3 cup to Basic Muffins recipe. Stir in 1 cup fresh blueberries or 3/4 cup canned blueberries, well drained, just before filling muffin tins.

Graham Muffins

Cut all-purpose flour in basic recipe to 1 cup and add 1 cup graham flour.

12 muffins

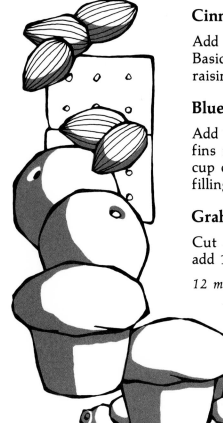

DATE NUT BREAD

Grease and flour an 8×4-inch loaf pan. Pour boiling water over dates; let cool. Cream shortening and sugar; add egg and vanilla and mix well. Sift dry ingredients together and add to shortening-sugar mixture in two batches alternately with 1/3 cup water. Blend in dates and nuts. Pour into prepared pan and bake in center of preheated convection oven on rack position 2 at 325° for 50 to 60 minutes, or until cake tester inserted in center comes out clean. Cool 15 minutes and remove to wire rack to cool completely.

1 loaf

1 cup boiling water
1 1/2 cups chopped, pitted dates
1/4 cup shortening
1/2 cup firmly packed brown sugar
1 egg
1 teaspoon vanilla extract
2 cups all-purpose flour
1 teaspoon baking soda
1 teaspoon baking powder
1 teaspoon salt
3/4 cup chopped walnuts

COOL-RISE DINNER ROLLS

Combine sugar, salt, yeast, and 2 cups flour in large bowl of electric mixer. Heat milk, 1 1/4 cups water, and butter in small saucepan on medium heat until very warm (120° to 130°). With mixer at low speed, gradually add liquid to dry ingredients. Beat 2 minutes at medium speed, scraping sides of bowl often. Add egg and 3/4 cup flour and beat at high speed for 2 minutes. Stir in enough additional flour to make a soft dough. Turn out on lightly floured surface and knead 10 minutes. Cover with plastic wrap and towel; let rise in a warm place (85°) for 20 minutes. Punch dough down; divide into 3 pieces. Cut each piece into 10 parts. Shape each into a ball. Place in greased 15 1/2×10 1/2×1-inch baking pan. Brush each roll with vegetable oil. Cover loosely with plastic wrap. Refrigerate at least 2 hours or overnight. When ready to bake, remove pan from refrigerator; uncover rolls carefully. Let stand at room temperature 10 minutes. Bake in preheated convection oven on rack position 1 at 350° for 20 to 25 minutes, or until browned. Remove from pans immediately and brush with melted butter and serve.

30 rolls

1/2 cup sugar
2 teaspoons salt
2 packages active dry yeast
5 1/2 to 6 1/2 cups all-purpose flour, divided
1/2 cup milk
1/2 cup butter or margarine
1 egg, at room temperature
Melted butter (optional)

FRENCH BREAD

Combine 1 1/2 cups flour, salt, and yeast in large bowl of electric mixer. Gradually add 1 1/4 cups hot tap water (120° to 130°) to flour mixture and beat 2 minutes at medium speed. Add 1/2 cup flour and beat 2 minutes at high speed. Stir in enough additional flour to make a stiff dough. Turn out onto lightly floured surface and knead 8 to 10 minutes. Place dough in bowl greased with butter. Turn to grease on all sides. Cover with towel and let rise in warm place (85°) until doubled in bulk, about 1 hour. Punch down. Turn onto lightly floured surface and let rest, covered, 15 minutes. Prepare French bread pan or cookie sheet by greasing and sprinkling with cornmeal. Divide dough into 2 parts and roll each into a 12×8-inch rectangle. Roll up jelly-roll fashion. Pinch ends to seal. Gently roll dough back and forth to lengthen roll. Place in prepared pan. Make 1/4-inch deep slashes in each loaf with a razor blade. Brush with egg white lightly beaten with 2 teaspoons cold water. Let rise, uncovered, in warm place until doubled, about 1 hour. Brush loaves again. Bake in a preheated convection oven on rack position 2 at 400° for 30 to 35 minutes, brushing loaves again after first 3 minutes in oven. Remove loaves from pan and place directly on oven rack for 3 minutes to crisp bottom of loaf if necessary.

3 to 4 cups all-purpose flour, divided
1 1/2 teaspoons salt
1 package active dry yeast
2 tablespoons cornmeal
1 egg white

2 16-inch loaves

VARIATION:

French Dinner Rolls

Follow recipe for French bread; divide dough into 8 parts. Form each part into a 6-inch roll. Proceed as for French bread. Bake 20 to 25 minutes at 400°.

8 6-inch rolls

Date Nut Bread (page 145)
French Bread
Cool-Rise Dinner Rolls (page 145)
Sesame Seed Bread Sticks (page 152)
Pita Bread (page 148)
Double Corn Sticks (page 141)

RAISIN BREAD

1 package active dry
    yeast
1/2 cup warm water
    (105° to 115°)
4 1/2 to 5 1/2 cups all-purpose
    flour, divided
1/4 cup sugar
1 teaspoon salt
1/4 cup butter or
    margarine, softened
1 1/4 cups raisins
3 teaspoons cinnamon
3 eggs
1 cup dairy sour cream
    or yogurt

Dissolve yeast in warm water. Combine 3 cups of flour, sugar, salt, and butter in large bowl. Mix raisins and cinnamon; add to flour mixture along with eggs, sour cream, and dissolved yeast. Mix thoroughly. Beat in enough flour to make a soft dough. Turn out onto lightly floured surface and knead 8 to 10 times. Place dough in greased bowl and turn in bowl to coat on all sides. Cover and let rise in warm place (about 85°) until doubled in bulk. Punch down dough and shape into 2 loaves. Place in 2 greased 8 1/2×4 1/2-inch bread pans. Cover and let rise until doubled in bulk, about 1 hour. Bake on rack position 2 in convection oven at 350° for 35 to 40 minutes. Remove from pans and cool on wire racks.

2 loaves

PITA BREAD

5 to 6 cups all-purpose
    flour, divided
1 tablespoon sugar
1 teaspoon salt
1 package active dry
    yeast
1/2 cup milk

Combine 3 cups flour, sugar, salt, and yeast in large bowl of electric mixer. Combine 1 1/2 cups water and milk in saucepan; heat to very warm (120° to 130°). Gradually add liquid to dry ingredients. Beat 2 minutes at medium speed with electric mixer. Stir in enough additional flour to make a soft dough. Turn out onto a lightly floured surface and knead 8 to 10 minutes. Place in greased bowl and turn to grease top of dough. Cover and let rise in a warm place (85°) until doubled in bulk. Punch dough down. Divide dough into 6 pieces. Roll each piece into an 8-inch circle, exactly 1/4 inch thick. Place on greased cookie sheets. Cover and let rise until exactly 1/2 inch thick. Preheat convection oven to 450°. Place cookie sheet, centered, on rack position 2. (Do 1 sheet at a time.) Bake 5 to 6 minutes. Tops may be browned further in the broiler, but watch very carefully.

6 pita breads

BEEF OR HAM PITA SANDWICHES

Combine mayonnaise, mustard, and onion in small bowl. Spread generously on each slice of meat. Roll meat around cheese. Cut each pita in half and open the pocket. Fill with the meat/cheese combination. Stand sandwiches in a small baking pan, cut side up. Bake in convection oven on rack position 2 at 300° for 15 minutes, or until meat is hot and cheese melted.

4 sandwiches

1/2 cup mayonnaise
2 tablespoons spicy brown mustard
1 teaspoon minced onion
4 slices lean roast beef and 4 slices Muenster cheese
or
4 thin slices cooked ham and 4 slices Swiss cheese
2 pita breads

CHEESE BREAD

Combine 2 1/2 cups flour, sugar, salt, and yeast in large bowl of electric mixer. Heat milk, 1 cup water, and cheese over medium heat until very warm (120° to 130°). With mixer at low speed, beat liquid into dry ingredients. Increase speed to medium and beat 2 minutes. Blend in 1/2 cup flour and beat at high speed 2 minutes. Stir in enough additional flour to make a soft dough. Turn out onto lightly floured surface and knead 8 to 10 minutes. Place dough in greased bowl and turn to grease top. Cover with towel and let rise in warm place (about 85°) until doubled in bulk, about 1 hour. Punch dough down and cut in half. Roll each half into a 12×8-inch rectangle. Roll up jelly-roll fashion. Press ends to seal. Place in 2 greased 9×5-inch loaf pans, seam side down. Cover, let rise in warm place until doubled in bulk, about 1 hour. Bake in preheated convection oven on rack position 2 at 350° for 30 to 35 minutes. Cool for 15 minutes in pans and remove to wire rack to cool completely.

2 loaves

3 1/2 to 4 cups all-purpose flour, divided
1/4 cup sugar
2 teaspoons salt
2 packages active dry yeast
3/4 cup milk
2 cups (8 ounces) shredded Cheddar cheese

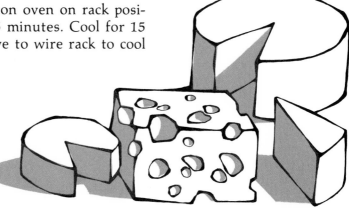

1 tablespoon salt
2/3 cup sugar
3 tablespoons butter or
   margarine
3 packages active dry yeast
7 to 7 1/2 cups all-purpose
   flour
2 eggs, beaten

WHITE BREAD

Combine 2 1/3 cups of water, salt, sugar, and margarine in a saucepan and heat to 115°. Add yeast and stir until dissolved. In a large bowl combine 5 cups of flour with the yeast mixture and the beaten eggs. Work in another 2 to 2 1/2 cups of flour. The dough should be sticky but firm. Place dough in a very large greased bowl and turn in bowl to coat on all sides. Cover with plastic wrap and secure with a rubber band. Place in refrigerator to rise overnight. The next day punch down dough and shape into 3 loaves. Place in 3 greased 8 1/2×4 1/2-inch loaf pans. Cover and let rise in a warm place until doubled in bulk, about 2 hours. Bake in preheated convection oven on rack position 2 at 350° for 30 to 40 minutes or until bread sounds hollow when tapped. Remove from pans and cool on wire racks.

3 loaves

VARIATION:

Caramel Pecan Rolls

Follow recipe for white bread. Set aside 1/2 recipe for rolls. Form other half into two small loaves and bake in preheated convection oven at 350° on rack position 2 for 30 minutes. Remove from pans and cool on racks.

To make rolls combine 1/3 cup honey, 1/2 cup firmly packed brown sugar, 1/4 cup butter or margarine, and 1/4 teaspoon salt in large saucepan. Heat to 234° or until soft ball forms in cold water. Spread mixture evenly in bottom of a well-greased 13×9-inch pan; sprinkle with 3/4 cup chopped pecans. On floured surface, roll reserved half of dough into 24×10-inch rectangle; brush with 3 tablespoons of melted butter. Combine 1/4 cup firmly packed brown sugar, and 1 1/2 teaspoons cinnamon, and 1/4 cup chopped pecans; sprinkle on dough. Roll dough jelly-roll fashion; cut into 16 even slices. Place rolls, cut side down, over caramel-nut mixture. Cover and let rise in warm place until doubled in bulk, 45 to 60 minutes. Preheat convection oven to 350°. Bake on rack position 2 for 25 to 30 minutes. Invert from pan and serve hot, or cool on wire racks.

16 rolls

OATMEAL BREAD

Combine milk, 3/4 cup water, margarine, and sugar, and heat until very warm (105° to 115°). Blend 2 cups flour and salt and combine with the milk mixture; beat 2 minutes at medium speed of electric mixer. Blend 1 cup flour with yeast, add to batter, and beat two minutes longer. By hand, beat in oats and enough flour to make a stiff dough. Turn out on floured surface; knead about 8 to 10 minutes. Place in greased bowl and turn to grease on all sides. Cover and let rise until double in bulk, about 1 hour. Punch down dough and divide in half. Shape into 2 loaves and place in greased 8 1/2×4 1/2-inch loaf pans. Brush tops with oil. Cover and let rise until doubled in size, about 1 hour. Bake in preheated convection oven on rack position 2 at 350° for 35 to 40 minutes. Remove from pans and cool on wire racks.

1 1/2 cups milk
1/4 cup butter or margarine
1/3 cup firmly packed brown sugar
5 1/3 to 5 2/3 cups all-purpose flour
2 teaspoons salt
2 packages active dry yeast
2 cups uncooked quick oats

2 loaves

PULL APART BREAD RING

Combine milk, 1/3 cup butter, sugar, and salt, and heat until butter is melted. Cool to 115° and stir in yeast until dissolved. Thoroughly mix flour and cooled liquid in a large bowl. Cover and let rise until doubled in bulk, about 1 1/2 hours. Turn dough out on a floured surface and roll to 1/2-inch thickness. Cut into 3-inch squares; dip each square into remaining 1/3 cup butter. Layer squares in a 10-inch bundt pan. Cover and let rise until doubled in bulk, about 35 to 45 minutes. Bake in preheated convection oven on rack position 2 at 350° for 30 to 35 minutes.

1 cup milk
2/3 cup butter or margarine, melted and divided
1/4 cup sugar
1 teaspoon salt
1 package active dry yeast
3 1/2 cups all-purpose flour

VARIATION:

Follow recipe for Pull Apart Bread Ring, adding 2 cloves garlic, grated, and 1/2 teaspoon thyme to the melted butter before dipping of dough squares in butter.

1 ring

HONEY WHEAT BREAD

2 packages active dry
   yeast
1 3/4 cups warm water
   (105° to 115°)
1 teaspoon salt
1/4 cup oil
1/4 cup firmly packed
   brown sugar
1/3 cup honey
2 1/2 cups whole wheat
   flour
1/3 cup regular wheat germ
3 to 3 1/2 cups all-purpose
   flour

In a large bowl dissolve yeast in warm water. Add salt, oil, brown sugar, and honey, and mix thoroughly. Stir in whole wheat flour, wheat germ, and 2 cups of all-purpose flour. Turn dough out on floured board and work in the remaining 1 to 1 1/2 cups of flour. Knead 10 minutes, place in greased bowl and turn to coat on all sides. Cover and let rise until doubled in bulk, 1 to 2 hours. Punch down and shape into 2 loaves. Place in 2 greased 8 1/2×4 1/2-inch loaf pans. Cover and let rise until doubled in bulk, about 1 hour. Bake in center of preheated convection oven on rack position 2 at 350° for 30 to 40 minutes. Remove from pans and cool on wire racks.

2 loaves

SESAME SEED BREAD STICKS

3 1/2 to 4 cups all-purpose
   flour, divided
3/4 teaspoon salt
1/2 teaspoon sugar
1 package active dry
   yeast
3 tablespoons butter or
   margarine
1 egg white, slightly
   beaten
1/3 cup sesame seed

Combine 1 1/2 cups flour, salt, sugar, and yeast in large bowl of electric mixer. Place 1 1/4 cups water and butter in saucepan and heat until very warm (120° to 130°). Gradually add liquid to dry ingredients and beat 2 minutes at medium speed. Stir in 1/2 cup flour and beat at high speed 2 minutes. Stir in enough additional flour to make a soft dough. Turn out onto lightly floured surface and knead 8 to 10 minutes. Place dough in greased bowl and turn to grease top. Cover and let rise in warm place (85°) until doubled in bulk, about 1 hour. Punch dough down and divide in half. Cut each half into 12 pieces and roll each into a rope 6 inches long. Place on greased cookie sheet, about 2 inches apart. Brush with beaten egg white and sprinkle with sesame seed. Cover, let rise until doubled, about 30 minutes. Preheat convection oven to 400°. Place cookie sheet on rack position 2. If 2 cookie sheets are available use rack positions 2 and 3. Bake 12 to 15 minutes. Rotate cookie sheets after 8 minutes. Remove to wire cake racks to cool.

24 bread sticks

HOT HERBED LOAF

Cut bread diagonally into 1-inch slices keeping slices in order. Blend butter, parsley, oregano, dillweed, and garlic. Spread bread slices with butter mixture and put slices together. Shape a rectangle of aluminum foil around the bottom and sides of the loaf but leave the top open. Spread top with any remaining butter. Turn on convection oven to 400°. Sprinkle generously with more parsley and Parmesan cheese. Bake on rack position 2 for about 10 minutes.

Note: This bread may be prepared hours ahead. Store tightly wrapped. Standing develops flavor.

8 to 10 servings

1 loaf French bread
1/2 cup butter or margarine, softened
1 teaspoon dry parsley
1/2 teaspoon oregano, crushed
1/4 teaspoon dillweed, crushed
1 clove garlic, crushed, or 2 teaspoons minced dry garlic
Grated Parmesan cheese

SOUR CREAM COFFEE CAKE

Cream butter and sugar. Add the eggs, one at a time, beating well after each addition. Combine the sour cream and vanilla, and add to batter alternately with flour, baking soda, cardamom, and salt. Mix until ingredients are combined. Grease and flour a 10-inch tube pan. Combine the pecans, cinnamon and sugar; sprinkle 1/3 of mixture over bottom of pan. Spoon in the batter and sprinkle with 1/2 of the remaining sugar-nut mixture; swirl into batter with knife. Top batter with the remaining sugar mixture and press in lightly. Bake in preheated 325° convection oven on rack position 2 for 60 to 65 minutes. Invert and cool on wire rack.

1 cake

1 cup butter or margarine
1 1/2 cups sugar
2 eggs
1 cup dairy sour cream
1 teaspoon vanilla extract
2 cups all-purpose flour
1/2 teaspoon baking soda
1/2 teaspoon cardamom optional
1/2 teaspoon salt
3/4 cup chopped pecans
2 teaspoons cinnamon
1/3 cup firmly packed brown sugar

DESSERTS

ALMOND-PEARS IN SWEET WINE

Lightly butter a shallow 9-inch round glass baking dish. Combine orange juice, lemon peel, vermouth, and preserves in a medium-size saucepan. Bring to a boil over medium heat, stirring constantly. Place pears in prepared dish. Pour sauce over pears and sprinkle with chopped almonds and macaroon crumbs. Cover loosely with foil and bake in convection oven on rack position 2 at 350° for 30 minutes; uncover, baste, and continue baking for another 10 minutes, uncovered, or until pears are fork tender. Serve slightly warm or at room temperature.

Another way: Substitute apricot preserves or orange marmalade for the peach preserves.

Note: The amount of time it will take to cook pears will depend on how ripe the pears are. Adjust cooking time accordingly.

6 servings

1/3 cup orange juice
   Grated peel of 1/2 lemon
1/3 cup sweet vermouth
2/3 cup peach preserves
  6 medium-size whole
      pears, peeled
      and cored
      from the bottom
1/4 cup finely chopped
      almonds
2/3 cup crushed almond
      macaroons or other
      crisp cookies

GLAZED BAKED APPLES

Wash apples, core to within 1/2 inch of bottom. Peel 1/3 of skin from top of each apple. Combine raisins, sugar, nuts, and cinnamon in small bowl. Fill center of apples with raisin mixture. Arrange apples in shallow baking dish. Combine corn syrup and food coloring. Pour over apples. Cover pan with foil; bake in center of convection oven on rack position 2 at 375° for 30 minutes. Remove cover, bake an additional 20 minutes, basting with syrup often. Cool slightly and serve with cream.

6 servings

  6 medium-size
      baking apples
  2 tablespoons raisins
  2 tablespoons firmly
      packed brown sugar
1/4 cup chopped walnuts
1/4 teaspoon cinnamon
3/4 cup light corn syrup
   Few drops red food
      coloring (optional)

Almond-Pears in Sweet Wine

FRUIT LEATHER

2 cups fruit purée
Dash salt

To prepare fruit purée, wash and dry fruit, remove pits or cores and any blemishes; cut in chunks and process a few at a time in the blender or with the chopping blade in a food processor. Add a dash of salt to the fruit. Lightly grease a 10×15×1-inch jelly-roll pan. Spread the fruit purée in it evenly to a depth of 1/4 inch. Bake in convection oven on rack position 1 or 2 at 175° for 3 to 7 hours, or until fruit leather is dry enough to be peeled from pan. Check often after 3 hours. When leather is done, roll up and cut into 1-inch slices and store at room temperature in an airtight container.

12 to 16 servings

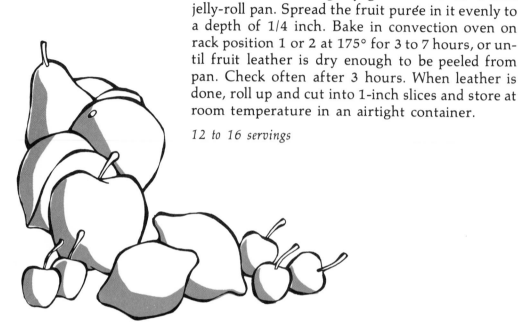

ANGEL FOOD CAKE

12 egg whites
   (about 1 1/2 cups)
1 teaspoon cream of
   tartar
1/2 teaspoon salt
1 1/4 cups sugar
1 cup cake flour
1/2 cup confectioners
   sugar
1 teaspoon vanilla
   extract

Place egg whites in large electric mixer bowl. Let stand until they come to room temperature. Add cream of tartar and salt. Beat at medium speed until frothy. Increase speed to high and gradually add sugar. Continue beating until sugar is dissolved. (Test by rubbing a little of the beaten egg whites between your fingers; when the graininess is gone, the sugar has dissolved.) Combine cake flour and confectioners sugar. Sift flour mixture over beaten egg whites and fold in gently with a rubber spatula. Fold in vanilla. Push batter into an ungreased 10-inch tube pan. Preheat convection oven to 325°. Bake on rack position 1 for 35 minutes, or until top is well browned and crusty. Remove from oven and invert cake on a narrow-necked bottle to cool completely. Remove cake from pan by loosening sides and tube with a long metal spatula.

1 cake

COCONUT POUND CAKE

Bring all ingredients to room temperature. Cream butter and shortening well. Gradually add sugar and beat until light and fluffy. Add eggs, one at a time, beating well after each addition. Combine sour cream, milk, lemon extract, and vanilla extract. Mix flour and baking powder. Add flour mixture and sour cream mixture alternately to batter, beginning and ending with the flour. Don't overbeat. Stir in coconut. Pour batter into a greased and floured 10-inch tube pan. Bake in preheated 325° convection oven on rack position 2 for 75 to 80 minutes.

1 cake

1	cup butter or margarine
1/3	cup shortening
2	cups sugar
5	large eggs
1	cup dairy sour cream
1/4	cup milk
1	teaspoon lemon extract
1	teaspoon vanilla extract
3	cups all-purpose flour
1/2	teaspoon baking powder
1	cup flaked coconut

COCONUT GINGER CAKE

Grease 9×9-inch pan. Sift flour, ginger, cinnamon, baking soda, and salt together. Cream sugar and butter in large mixing bowl. Beat in eggs. Combine molasses, and 1/2 cup water; add alternately with dry ingredients to egg mixture and mix well. Add coconut and mix. Pour batter into prepared pan. Bake in preheated convection oven on rack position 2 at 325° for 35 minutes, or until cake tester inserted in center comes out clean. Serve warm or cold. Nice with warm Lemon Sauce.

8 servings

1 3/4	cups all-purpose flour
1	teaspoon ginger
1	teaspoon cinnamon
1	teaspoon baking soda
1/8	teaspoon salt
1/2	cup sugar
1/2	cup butter or margarine
2	eggs
1/2	cup molasses
1	can (3 1/2 ounces) moist shredded coconut

Lemon Sauce

Mix thoroughly and cook over low heat, stirring constantly, until slightly thick. Serve hot.

Note: Add 1 tablespoon cornstarch to this recipe to make a piquant filling for layer cake or cream puffs.

Lemon Sauce

1/2	cup sugar
2	tablespoons cornstarch
1	cup boiling water
2	or 3 tablespoons lemon juice
1	egg
	Pinch salt

CHANTILLY TORTE

Grease and flour two 9-inch round cake pans. Combine flour, baking powder, and salt; set aside. In a large bowl, combine butter and 1/2 cup sugar, and beat until creamy. Add egg yolks, one at a time, beating well after each addition. Blend in almond extract and milk. Fold in flour mixture. Spread in prepared pans; set aside. Beat egg whites in small bowl until foamy. Gradually add remaining 1/2 cup sugar and beat until stiff peaks form. Spread over cake batter. Sprinkle with almonds. Bake in center of preheated convection oven on rack position 2 at 325° for 25 minutes. Cool 5 minutes, then turn out, meringue side up. Cool completely.

Beat cream with confectioners sugar until soft peaks form. Place 1 cake layer on serving platter. Spread with half the cream mixture and half the strawberries. Place the remaining cake layer on top and repeat with the cream and strawberries. Refrigerate until ready to serve.

8 to 10 servings

- 1 cup all-purpose flour
- 1 teaspoon baking powder
- 1/4 teaspoon salt
- 1/2 cup butter, softened
- 1 cup sugar, divided
- 5 eggs, separated
- 1/2 teaspoon almond extract
- 3 tablespoons milk
- 1/2 cup slivered almonds
- 2 cups heavy cream
- 2 tablespoons confectioners sugar
- 1 pint fresh strawberries, hulled and sliced

WALNUT DESSERT ROLL

Generously grease and flour a 15×10×1-inch baking pan. Beat eggs and sugar in large bowl until thick and lemon-colored. Fold in walnuts, bread crumbs, flour, vanilla, and salt. Pour into prepared pan. Preheat convection oven to 325°. Bake on rack position 2 for 15 to 18 minutes. Immediately invert onto dish towel coated with confectioners sugar. Carefully roll as for jelly roll. Cool on wire rack. Meanwhile, combine heavy cream, brandy, and 2 tablespoons confectioners sugar in small bowl. Beat until soft peaks form. Unwrap cooled walnut roll carefully and spread with cream; roll again. Sprinkle with confectioners sugar and remove to serving platter.

6 servings

- 4 eggs
- 2/3 cup sugar
- 1 cup ground walnuts
- 1/2 cup dry bread crumbs
- 1/4 cup all-purpose flour
- 1 teaspoon vanilla extract
  Dash salt
- 1 cup heavy cream
- 2 tablespoons brandy
  Confectioners sugar

Chantilly Torte

CHOCOLATE ECLAIRS

1/2 cup butter
1/4 teaspoon salt
1 cup all-purpose flour
4 eggs, at room
   temperature
Vanilla Cream Filling
Chocolate Glaze

Combine 1 cup of water, butter, and salt in a saucepan; heat to a full boil. Reduce heat and add flour all at once, stirring vigorously until mixture leaves sides of the pan. Remove from heat. Add eggs, one at a time, beating well after each addition. Preheat convection oven to 375°. Press dough through pastry tube or shape with spoon into 4x1-inch fingers and place on greased baking sheet. Place baking sheet on rack position 2. Bake at 375° for 35 to 40 minutes, or until golden. Cool on wire racks. Cut eclairs in half horizontally. Spoon Vanilla Cream Filling or whipped cream into the bottom half of eclairs and replace tops. Glaze with Chocolate Glaze.

16 eclairs

Nice to know: If you want to put your food processor to good use, place the cooked batter in the food processor bowl with cutting blade in place. Cover bowl, turn machine on, and add eggs one at a time. Process after each egg is added until blended.

Vanilla Cream Filling

1/2 cup sugar
1/4 cup cornstarch
1/8 teaspoon salt
2 3/4 cups milk
2 eggs, beaten
2 tablespoons butter or
   margarine
1 teaspoon vanilla
   extract

Combine sugar, cornstarch, and salt in a saucepan. Gradually stir in milk. Stirring constantly, bring to a boil over medium heat and boil for 1 minute. Blend a small amount of the mixture into beaten eggs. Return all to saucepan. Cook over low heat, stirring constantly, about 5 minutes. Remove from heat; blend in butter and vanilla.

Chocolate Glaze

1/2 package (6 ounces)
   semi-sweet chocolate
   pieces
1/2 teaspoon shortening

Over hot (not boiling) water, melt chocolate and shortening. Glaze filled eclairs.

GINGERBREAD

Grease and flour a 9-inch square baking pan. Measure all ingredients into large bowl of electric mixer; add 2/3 cup hot tap water; blend at low speed until well mixed. Increase speed to medium and beat 2 minutes. Pour batter into prepared pan. Bake in center of preheated convection oven on rack position 2 at 325° for 40 minutes. Cool cake in pan on wire rack. Cut in squares and serve with brandied hard sauce, applesauce, or flavored whipped cream.

16 servings

2 1/2 cups all-purpose flour
2/3 cup molasses
1/2 cup firmly packed dark brown sugar
2/3 cup shortening
2 eggs
1 teaspoon baking soda
1 teaspoon cinnamon
1 teaspoon ginger
3/4 teaspoon salt
1/2 teaspoon baking powder
1/2 teaspoon allspice

CHEESE STRUDEL

Combine ricotta, sugar, egg, flour, lemon peel, and raisins in small bowl; set aside. Unwrap phyllo leaves carefully. Remove 3 leaves, rewrap, and refrigerate remaining leaves to use at another time. Place 1 leaf on a damp dish towel as the package directs. Place remaining 2 phyllo leaves between damp dish towels. Brush with melted butter. Sprinkle wth bread crumbs. Place second leaf over first and repeat butter and bread crumbs. Place third leaf on top. Spoon cheese mixture in a 3-inch strip down length of leaves. Roll up jelly-roll fashion with the aid of the dish towel. Place on greased cookie sheet. Brush with melted butter. Place cookie sheet on rack position 2. Bake in convection oven at 350° 25 to 30 minutes, or until golden. Cool on cookie sheet and serve sprinkled with confectioners sugar.

6 servings

1 cup ricotta cheese
1/4 cup sugar
1 egg
1 tablespoon all-purpose flour
1 teaspoon grated lemon peel
1/4 cup raisins
3 phyllo leaves
3 tablespoons butter or margarine, melted, divided
3 tablespoons dry bread crumbs
Confectioners sugar (optional)

PEACH CRISP

4 cups sliced, peeled
    peaches
1/2 cup sugar
3/4 teaspoon cinnamon
3/4 cup plus 2 tablespoons
    all-purpose flour,
    divided
1/3 cup butter
    or margarine
1/3 cup firmly packed
    brown sugar

Combine peaches with sugar, cinnamon, and 2 tablespoons of flour; place in 8-inch square pan. Combine 3/4 cup flour with brown sugar. Cut in butter with a pastry blender or two knives until mixture resembles coarse meal. Sprinkle mixture over peaches. Bake in center of convection oven on rack position 2 at 350° for 35 to 40 minutes. Cool slightly and serve with sweetened whipped cream or dairy sour cream.

4 servings

BLUEBERRY COBBLER

4 cups fresh or frozen
    blueberries, thawed
4 teaspoons tapioca
1 tablespoon lemon juice
1/2 cup plus 2
    tablespoons sugar,
    divided
1 cup all-purpose
    flour
1 1/2 teaspoons baking
    powder
1/4 teaspoon salt
1/8 teaspoon nutmeg
1/4 cup butter or
    margarine
1/4 cup milk
1 egg

Combine blueberries, 1/2 cup water, tapioca, lemon juice, and 1/2 cup sugar in a saucepan; bring to a boil. Pour into 1 1/2-quart casserole. Combine flour, 2 tablespoons sugar, baking powder, salt, and nutmeg in a small bowl. Cut in butter with a pastry blender or two knives until mixture resembles coarse crumbs. Add milk and egg and stir to combine. Drop mixture by spoonfuls on top of berry mixture. Bake in center of preheated convection oven, on rack position 2 at 400° for 20 to 25 minutes. Cool slightly.

6 servings

COUNTRY APPLE PIE

6 cups thinly sliced
    cooking apples,
    such as McIntosh or
    Greenings
    Pastry for 9-inch pie,
    unbaked
1/2 cup sugar
1/4 cup firmly packed
    brown sugar
1/4 cup all-purpose flour
1/2 teaspoon nutmeg
1/2 teapsoon cinnamon,
    divided
    Dash salt
2 tablespoons lemon juce
2/3 cup dairy sour cream
1 tablespoon sugar

Arrange apple slices in pie shell. Combine sugar, brown sugar, flour, nutmeg, 1/4 teaspoon cinnamon, and salt in a bowl. Combine remaining cinnamon and sugar; sprinkle over apples. Cover pie with foil. Bake in center of convection oven on rack position 1 at 400° for 30 minutes. Remove foil and bake an additional 20 to 25 minutes. Serve warm.

Note: Hearty cheddar cheese is the traditional accompaniment for warm apple pie, but for a different taste, try mellow Jarlsberg or Double Glouster instead.

8 servings

Country Apple Pie

CHEESE PIE

2 packages (8 ounces
    each) cream cheese,
    at room temperature
1/2 cup sugar
2 eggs
1 teaspoon vanilla extract
1 3/4 cups dairy sour
    cream, divided
1 9-inch graham cracker
    pie crust, unbaked
    Cinnamon

Beat cream cheese and sugar in large bowl until creamy. Blend in eggs and vanilla. Fold in 1 cup sour cream. Pour into prepared graham cracker crust. Bake in convection oven on rack position 2 at 325° for 35 to 40 minutes. Remove from oven and spread remaining sour cream on top of pie. Sprinkle with cinnamon. Return to oven and bake an additional 10 minutes. Chill several hours before serving.

8 servings

CUSTARD PIE

Place pastry in pie pan or fluted dish. In the top of a double boiler, lightly beat together the other ingredients. Let the custard mixture get warm, not hot. Strain into pastry. Bake in convection oven on rack position 1 at 425° for 10 minutes, then reduce temperature to 325° and bake about 10 to 15 minutes longer. Watch the pie carefully during the last 5 minutes of cooking; the filling should be quite firm around the edges but still a little soft in the middle since it will continue to cook after it is removed from the oven. Let stand 30 minutes before serving. Custard pie should always be stored in the refrigerator, tightly covered, but it is best eaten when it reaches room temperature the first time.

Pastry for
  1 single-crust
  9-inch pie, unbaked
3 eggs
1/4 cup sugar
1 teaspoon vanilla
  extract
1 1/2 cups light cream
Pinch salt
1/4 teaspoon nutmeg

VARIATIONS:

Raisin Pie

Follow recipe for Custard Pie but reduce cream to 1 cup and add 1 cup plumped raisins to filling. Plump raisins by letting them stand in a strainer over boiling water for 5 minutes. Dry on paper towels before adding to pie.

Caramel Pie

Follow recipe for Custard Pie but substitute 3/4 cup dark brown sugar for sugar. Maple flavoring (1 teaspoon) may be substituted for the nutmeg.

Rhubarb-Strawberry Pie

Follow recipe for Custard Pie but use 1 cup sugar and add 1 cup each of sliced fresh rhubarb cut into 1/4-inch slices and sliced strawberries. Reduce cream to 3/4 cup. A lattice top crust is very attractive on this pie.

Currant Pie

Follow recipe for Custard Pie but use 1 cup sugar and add 1 cup fresh red or black currants (the berries, not the dried grape product). Reduce cream to 1 cup.

6 servings

WALNUT ICE CREAM PIE

1 egg white
1/4 teaspoon salt
1/4 cup sugar
1/2 cup finely chopped
walnuts
1 quart vanilla
ice cream

Beat egg white with salt until stiff. Beat in sugar, 1 tablespoon at a time, until soft peaks form. Fold in walnuts. Butter a 9-inch pie pan; spoon in mixture. Shape with back of spoon to form shell. Bake in convection oven on rack position 2 at 225° for 1 hour and 30 minutes. Cool. Fill with softened ice cream and freeze until hard. Serve with topping.

6 to 8 servings

Topping

3 tablespoons butter
3/4 cup firmly packed
brown sugar
1 teaspoon cornstarch
1/2 cup light cream or
evaporated milk
1/2 cup chopped walnuts

Melt butter on medium heat; add brown sugar and cornstarch. Remove from heat and slowly add cream. Return to heat; stir constantly for 1 minute. Add walnuts. Serve slightly warm topping on frozen pie.

FOOD PROCESSOR CRUMB CRUST

22 graham cracker
squares
1/4 cup sugar
1/3 cup butter or
margarine, softened

Place crackers in bowl of food processor with steel blade in position. Add sugar. Process until crackers are crumbed. Add butter and process until blended. Preheat convection oven to 350°. Pour crumbs into 8 or 9-inch pie plate and press firmly over bottom and sides. Bake pie shell 8 to 10 minutes on rack position 2. Pie shell may be frozen and baked for 10 to 12 minutes when needed.

1 8- or 9-inch pie shell

FOOD PROCESSOR PASTRY CRUST

2 cups all-purpose
flour
1 teaspoon salt
2/3 cup shortening,
chilled
1/4 cup very cold water

Measure flour and salt into bowl of food processor with steel blade in position. Break up shortening into small pieces. Process until the mixture resembles coarse meal. While continuing to process add the water through the chute. Process until a ball forms and leaves sides of bowl. Chill about 1/2 hour. Preheat convection oven to 450°. Roll out pastry for 8 or 9-inch pie. Bake 8 to 10 minutes on rack position 2. Pie shell may be frozen and baked for 10 to 12 minutes when needed.

1 8- or 9-inch pie shell

GRAND MARNIER SOUFFLE

Remove top rack of oven. Generously butter a 1 1/2-quart soufflé dish. Butter one side of long piece of aluminum foil. Make a 3-inch collar with buttered side facing in. Melt butter in saucepan; add flour and stir to make a roux. Gradually add milk and stir until thickened. Stir in orange peel and sugar. Heat until sugar dissolves. Slowly add a small amount of sauce base to beaten egg yolks, beating vigorously. Pour egg mixture back into saucepan slowly, beating constantly. Stir in vanilla and Grand Marnier. Transfer to large bowl and set aside. Preheat convection oven to 375°. Beat egg whites and salt in separate bowl until foamy. Add cream of tartar and sugar and beat until stiff peaks form. Gently fold egg whites into sauce. Fill prepared dish. Place in center of oven on rack position 1. Bake 25 to 30 minutes. Remove collar and serve immediately.

6 servings

- 2 1/2 tablespoons butter
- 3 tablespoons all-purpose flour
- 1 cup milk
- 1 tablespoon grated orange peel
- 6 tablespoons sugar
- 4 egg yolks, lightly beaten
- 2 teaspoons vanilla extract
- 1/3 cup Grand Marnier
- 5 egg whites, at room temperature
- Pinch salt
- 1/4 teaspoon cream of tartar
- 1 tablespoon sugar

BREAD PUDDING

Soak bread crumbs in milk. Add remaining ingredients and mix well. Pour into a buttered 8×8-inch square pan and bake in convection oven on rack position 2 at 350° for 40 minutes. The top should be browned and the center fairly firm.

6 servings

Nice to know: Serve with Lemon Sauce (page 157) or Hot Rum Sauce, recipe below.

- 2 cups fresh bread crumbs
- 2 cups milk
- 3 eggs, slightly beaten
- 1/2 cup sugar
- 1/4 cup butter or margarine, melted
- 1/2 teaspoon vanilla extract
- 1 cup shredded coconut
- 1/2 cup raisins

HOT RUM SAUCE

Mix sugar and flour in saucepan. Add butter and boiling water and blend. Bring to a boil, reduce heat and simmer 5 minutes. Remove from heat and add rum. Serve with Bread Pudding.

- 1 cup firmly packed brown sugar
- 2 teaspoons all-purpose flour
- 1/2 cup butter or margarine
- 1/2 cup boiling water
- 1/2 cup dark or light rum

CHOCOLATE AND VANILLA COOKIES

3 squares (1 ounce each) semi-sweet chocolate
1 1/2 cups all-purpose flour
1/2 teaspoon baking soda
1/4 teaspoon salt
1/3 cup butter or margarine, softened
1/3 cup sugar
1 egg
1/2 teaspoon vanilla extract
1/4 cup milk
Pecan or walnut halves

Melt chocolate over hot (not boiling) water; set aside. Combine flour, baking soda, and salt. Combine butter and sugar in large, separate bowl; beat until creamy. Blend in egg and vanilla. Alternately add flour mixture and milk to butter mixture. Divide dough in half. Blend melted chocolate into one half. Preheat convection oven to 350°. Drop vanilla dough by half teaspoonfuls onto greased cookie sheets. Drop half teaspoonful of chocolate dough next to vanilla, edges touching. Press nut half in center so half of nut is on vanilla dough and other half of nut is on chocolate dough. Place cookie sheet on rack position 2. Bake 6 to 8 minutes, or until done. Remove to wire rack to cool.

36 cookies

THUMBPRINT COOKIES

3/4 cup butter or margarine, softened
1/2 cup firmly packed brown sugar
1 egg, separated
1 teaspoon vanilla extract
1 1/4 cups all-purpose flour
1/4 teaspoon salt
1 1/2 cups chopped walnuts
1/4 cup raspberry or strawberry preserves

Beat butter and sugar in large bowl until creamy. Blend in egg yolk and vanilla. Gradually add flour and salt. Cover and chill at least 2 hours. Shape mixture into 1-inch balls. Dip each ball into slightly beaten egg white and roll in nuts. Place on ungreased cookie sheets. Preheat convection oven to 350°. Make a hole in center of each cookie with thumb. Fill with preserves. Place cookie sheets on rack position 2. Bake 10 to 12 minutes. Cool slightly, remove from cookie sheets, and place on rack to finish cooling.

24 to 30 cookies

Lemon Glazed Coconut Squares
Chocolate and Vanilla Cookies
Thumbprint Cookies (page 171)

PECAN FINGERS

1 cup butter or
   margarine, softened
1/4 cup confectioners
   sugar
1 egg
1 teaspoon vanilla extract
1 3/4 cups all-purpose flour
1/4 teaspoon salt
2 cups ground pecans

Combine butter and confectioners sugar in large bowl; beat until creamy. Add egg and vanilla. Gradually blend in flour and salt. Stir in pecans. Cover dough and chill at least 1 hour. Preheat convection oven to 350°. Form teaspoonfuls of dough into fingers 1/2×2 inches. Place on greased cookie sheet. Place cookie sheet on rack position 2. Bake 8 to 10 minutes, or until golden. Roll each cookie in confectioners sugar while still warm.

12 cookies

CHOCOLATE PECAN CRUNCHIES

1 ounce unsweetened
   baking chocolate
1/2 cup butter
3/4 cup sugar
1 egg, lightly beaten
1 teaspoon vanilla extract
1/3 cup all-purpose flour
1/4 teaspoon salt
3/4 cup chopped pecans,
   walnuts, or almonds

Melt chocolate over very low heat. Gradually add butter, stirring until smooth. Remove from heat, add sugar, egg, and vanilla. Stir well. Add flour and salt and stir to combine. Pour batter into greased 10×15-inch jellyroll pan, spreading evenly to cover entire pan. Sprinkle with nuts. Bake in convection oven at 350° on rack position 2 for 12 to 13 minutes. Run a knife along all edges of pan and cut cookies into squares as soon as pan comes from oven. Remove with spatula and cool on rack.

35 cookies

LAYERED CHEESE BROWNIES

2 packages (3 ounces
   each) cream cheese,
   at room temperature
3 eggs
1 cup sugar, divided
3/4 cup plus 2 tablespoons
   all-purpose flour,
   divided
1/2 teaspoon vanilla extract
1/2 teaspoon baking soda
1/2 teaspoon salt
1/2 cup milk
1/4 cup butter or
   margarine, softened
2 squares (1 ounce each)
   unsweetened chocolate,
   melted

Grease and flour one 9-inch square baking pan. Combine cream cheese, 2 eggs, 1/4 cup sugar, 2 tablespoons flour, and vanilla in small bowl; beat until creamy. Pour into prepared pan; set aside. Combine remaining 3/4 cup flour, remaining 3/4 cup sugar, baking soda and salt in large bowl. Blend in milk, butter, chocolate, and 1 egg. Spoon chocolate mixture over cheese mixture and run knife through to marbleize. Bake in center of preheated convection oven on rack position 2 at 350° for 25 to 30 minutes. Cool in pan on wire rack. Cut into squares to serve.

16 brownies

LEMON GLAZED COCONUT SQUARES

Combine flour, 2 tablespoons brown sugar, and salt. Cut in butter with pastry blender or two knives until mixture resembles coarse meal. Preheat convection oven to 350°. Press dough in bottom of 8- or 9-inch square baking pan. Bake in center of oven on rack position 2 for 10 minutes. Meanwhile, combine eggs and sugar in a small bowl; beat until foamy. Stir in nuts and coconut. Spread over baked layer. Return to oven and bake an additional 15 minutes. Cool slightly; spread with Lemon Glaze.

1 1/4 cups all-purpose flour
1/2 cup plus 2 tablespoons firmly packed brown sugar, divided
1/8 teaspoon salt
1/3 cup butter or margarine, softened
2 eggs
1/4 cup sugar
1/2 cup chopped pecans
1 cup shredded coconut

20 squares

Lemon Glaze

Combine confectioners sugar, lemon juice, and peel in small bowl. Blend well.

2/3 cup sifted confectioners sugar
1 tablespoon lemon juice
1/2 teaspoon grated lemon peel

PEANUT BUTTERSCOTCH BARS

1   egg
1   egg white
1/4   cup milk
1   teaspoon vanilla
        extract
1 1/2   cups firmly packed
        brown sugar
1/2   cup peanut butter
1/4   cup vegetable oil
2   cups all-purpose
        flour
2   teaspoons baking
        powder
1/2   teaspoon salt

Topping

1   egg yolk
1/4   cup peanut butter
2   tablespoons boiling
        water
1/2   cup confectioners
        sugar
3/4   cup chopped salted
        peanuts

Blend egg and egg white together in large mixing bowl; add milk, vanilla, sugar, peanut butter, and vegetable oil; mix well. Sift together flour, baking powder, and salt. Add to peanut butter mixture and mix well. Spread batter in greased 10×15-inch pan and bake in convection oven on rack position 2 at 350° for 18 to 20 minutes. While batter is baking, mix egg yolk, peanut butter, water, and sugar until smooth. While the cake is still very hot, spread topping on; sprinkle with chopped peanuts and cut into bars.

Note: Use a pastry brush to spread topping easily.

48 bars

INDEX